I NEVER
MET AN ANIMAL
I DIDN'T LIKE

I Never Met an Animal I Didn't Like

RORY C. FOSTER, DVM

FRANKLIN WATTS 1987
NEW YORK TORONTO

The names and identifying characteristics
of some of the individuals and places in
this book have been changed, but the book
is autobiographical in scope.

Library of Congress Cataloging-in-Publication Data

Foster, Rory C.
I never met an animal I didn't like.

1. Foster, Rory C. 2. Veterinarians—Wisconsin—
Biography. 3. Wildlife diseases—Treatment—
Wisconsin. I. Title.
SF996.4.F67A3 1987 636.089'092'4 [B] 86-28988
ISBN 0-531-15041-0

To all who suffer from
neuromuscular disorders,
and to their families
and their friends

FOREWORD

IT'S A WARM EARLY-FALL EVENING IN 1974. THE FLIGHT INTO the northern Wisconsin resort community of Rhinelander has just touched down, and the passengers are milling about the lobby of the airport. Unfamiliar eyes seek to make contact among the confusion of visitors. Somewhere in this group is a young man about to graduate from Michigan State's Veterinary School; he's here to be interviewed for his first job as a doctor of veterinary medicine.

Someone stepped forward. . . . "Are you Dr. Dunn?"

"Yes."

"Hi, I'm Rory Foster."

Having been a collegian in the not too distant past, I read his mind and almost reflexively made a suggestion: "Let's go have a beer."

I didn't know it at the time but that was the last I was to read the mind of this unusual individual. Looking back to our pre-employment "interview" that night, I'm often struck by how much Rory has done to change the lives of those who have known him . . . and how infinitely more has been his effect on so many living creatures who could not know him. And yet in their innocent ignorance they owe him so much.

During the twelve years that we were associated as friends and business partners, Rory always seemed to be one imaginative step ahead of me. Sharp as a tack, quick-witted, and possessed of an extraordinary sense of humor, he kept those around him in a continuous state of mental preparedness!

I'm reminded of Rory's first encounter with his wife, Linda, a lady of remarkable beauty and equally tender spirit. I happened to be examining her dog for a minor toe ailment when Rory got a glimpse of her on the way out the door. Never one to let an opportunity slip away, he said, "T.J., I don't care what was wrong with that dog. Just make sure it gets back in here for a recheck."

Three days later I summoned Dr. Foster into the exam room for his opinion on how to treat the now microscopically small, healing toe lesion. Three hours later he and Linda were having dinner and drinks! Smart guy, that Rory.

Always analytical, Rory would rather say, "Here's what I think" about a particular problem or conflict, than ask, "What do you think?" One morning Rory arrived at work in an exceptionally good mood, considering the day's case load. He had apparently made a discovery and wanted to share it with us. The announcement to the entire animal hospital staff went like this: "Life is what you make it, and what you make it depends totally on attitude. Attitude," he emphasized, "is the key."

Rory Foster's attitude toward the living creatures brought to him for care inspired him and Linda to establish a now highly regarded nonprofit wildlife rehabilitation center. A few thoughts from his first book, *Dr. Wildlife*, pointedly underscore his attitude toward nature's wilderness creatures. An injured rabbit was brought in for Dr. Foster's evaluation; his impressions follow:

> As had happened hundreds of times in the last five years, I had to make a decision about a wild animal's life. There were hundreds, thousands, maybe millions of exact replicas of this patient out in the wild. The life of this one tiny creature was unimportant to the overall rabbit population.
>
> I stood over the frightened little creature and began to list mentally all the arguments in favor of humane euthanasia. Decisions between my heart and my head have never been easy for me.
>
> I arrived home late, but Linda didn't mind at all. She even volunteered to get up during the night to help feed the new patient.

Considering the short time Rory Foster has spent in northern Wisconsin, his accomplishments are remarkable. Not the least of which is his terrific family, composed of Linda, daughters Ali and Rori Elizabeth, son Mike, three dogs, and two cats. Business enterprises conceived and brought to reality include a thriving mail-order outlet, partnership in numerous animal hospitals, a highly respected national newsletter, and widespread admiration for his first book.

Outside his family, I think the real jewel in the crown is the Northwoods Wildlife Hospital and Rehabilitation Center he and Linda founded in Minocqua, Wisconsin. This project was an outgrowth of Dr. Foster's keen interest in the birds and animals of the forest. The center will be a lasting tribute to the visionary man whose attitudes and energies helped reshape people's thinking regarding our voiceless wilderness friends.

Soaring freely on the summer thermals or hiding beneath the sheltering tamaracks are the offspring of creatures once broken and sick, healed by the hands of the helpers at the Wildlife Center. These woodland creatures sing their songs or flick their furry ears because of one man's imaginative and sympathetic attitude. They could never know Dr. Rory Foster. I did. And I'll miss him.

T. J. Dunn, DVM

ACKNOWLEDGMENTS

FIRST AND FOREMOST, I WISH TO THANK CAROL ERSEPKE FOR her encouraging and understanding assistance with the manuscript. Her excellent command of the English language, along with her thoughtful comments have definitely enhanced the writing.

Furthermore, I'd like to express my gratitude to Carol for her photographic talents, which are vividly displayed throughout the text. Even without so much as an accompanying word, her pictures would still tell a story. She's a professional in every sense of the word.

A special thank-you is owed to Jill Mode for the hours she spent typing and retyping the manuscript. Besides her technical skills, I appreciated her input into the preparation of *I Never Met an Animal I Didn't Like*. Her contagious laugh kept us all in good humor throughout this endeavor.

I'd also like to express my appreciation to Gail Kock for her unselfish assistance around the office. She's a very kind person and a good friend.

Lastly, my deepest gratitude goes to the creatures I've come to know through my veterinary work. They have taught me much.

Rory C. Foster, DVM

INTRODUCTION

I AM IN A SMALL LOG CABIN JUST OUTSIDE OF RHINELANDER, Wisconsin, as I write these words. Like a good friend, the fireplace eases the early autumn night chill. My wife, Linda, gets up now and again to feed the fire. The dried white bark from the birch logs burns like a torch, tossing phantom shadows across the knotty pine walls. A cozy cabin is one of the amenities of Northwoods life.

Our young children, Ali, Mike, and Rori Elizabeth, worn out from the day at the lake, have been asleep for the better part of two hours. Tenille, our ten-year-old golden retriever, slumbers at my feet. The odor of buttery popcorn, mixed with an occasional wisp of wood smoke that eludes the chimney, imparts a distinctive and pleasing fragrance to the room.

Linda and I are reminiscing about our days spent working with injured wildlife. Ten years before, shortly after we had married, we had settled in Minocqua, a small town about twenty-five miles to the north of our cabin. Together we started a veterinary hospital there. It was also there that my interest in wildlife medicine was kindled. As I recall, my first patient was a car-struck fawn. Then someone brought me an owl with a broken wing. Before too many months, and without specific design, our clinic was inundated with injured wild creatures from all over the region.

Treating and rehabilitating injured wildlife so they could be returned to their natural habitat was fascinating and very rewarding. But often my hospital, originally designed for doctoring dogs and cats, was not large enough to accommodate all of the wild animal patients. The need for a specialized building soon became evident. Consequently, the nonprofit organization I founded—the Northwoods Wildlife Hospital and Rehabilitation Center—constructed a new facility.

My 1985 book, *Dr. Wildlife*, chronicles this crusade to build the Midwest's first private wildlife hospital. Subsequent mail suggests something I suspected all along. There are many Dr. Wildlifes out there. It's heartening for me to have discovered that so very many are willing to lend a hand to help an injured wild creature.

But the Northwoods Wildlife Center, as it's now called, continues its work without me. Diagnosed about two years ago, at age thirty-three, with a debilitating motor neuron disease, my active involvement has been cut short. In fact, my practicing veterinary career appears to be over.

Faced with an uncertain future, Linda and I now spend more time looking back than ever before. That portion of our lives we shared working with the wildlings has taken on a new dimension. We realize now that we had been fueled by a special sense of mission.

Everyone has their own "good ol' days." These are ours.

I NEVER
MET AN ANIMAL
I DIDN'T LIKE

TENILLE

APPOINTMENTS NORMALLY LASTED UNTIL 6:00 P.M. AT OUR clinic in Minocqua. Occasionally, though, we finished earlier. July 27 was one of those days. I stayed behind to walk the dogs, treat the hospitalized cats, and lock up. Linda left at 5:40. This would give her a little extra time before dinner to take care of our fawn.

I was outside the kennel door with Brutus, a prodigious St. Bernard recovering from knee surgery, when I heard the phone ring.

"Come on," I urged my patient. I had to return inside to answer the phone. I tugged on the leash. Brutus sat down.

"Brutus, heel." The large dog rolled his eyes. He didn't know commands. The phone rang for the third time.

"Brutus!" I yelled in his ear. "Come on!" I pulled harder. He didn't move. I tied his leash to the doorknob and sprinted for the phone.

"Foster Animal Hospital. May I help you?"

"Dandelion got out of his pen," Linda blurted. I could tell that she was frantic and on the verge of tears.

"What do you mean—" I started, but Linda interrupted before I could finish.

"Dandelion is not in the pen. He's not in the yard either. I've looked all over," Linda nearly shouted.

My mind started to race. Dandelion was our two-month-old fawn which had been hit by a car a month earlier. Surgery had been necessary to repair his broken rear leg, and he still wore a cumbersome splint.

"How in the world did he get over the three-foot-high fence with his leg in a splint?" I thought out loud.

"I don't know how," Linda answered, "but I'm sure he's gone."

"I've just finished treatments. I'll be right home." I slammed the phone down and bolted for the kennel door.

"Brutus, you've got to come in. Now!" The big dog knew I was serious this time. He stood up and lumbered inside. "There, that wasn't so bad, was it?" I led him to his pen and closed the door behind him. On my way out of the clinic, I grabbed a paper towel and wiped his drool off my leg.

I ran across the gravel parking lot and leaped into my Bronco. I hadn't told Linda, but I knew the fawn had to be found. Dandelion was not only too young to survive on his own, but I knew the splint would eventually get wet. A wet splint on any animal always leads to an infection. Untreated infections of this sort can get into the bloodstream and be fatal. Even if this didn't happen, the splint would hinder Dandelion's ability to escape predators. Either way, the end would be the same.

The early evening sun temporarily blinded me as I turned west onto the highway. I stepped harder on the gas and thought about where the little fawn might go. We lived about six miles from the clinic, just off Highway 70 near Lake Shishebogama. The house was not large, but it was comfortable and it was our first. The weathered brown exterior blended perfectly with the surrounding woods. The house was built on a gently sloping ridge, of sorts. We didn't have much of what could be called a yard. There was some grass in front but none on the other three sides. There were simply trees, mixed hardwood— mostly oak, but with a few birch, maple, and pine scattered throughout. The trees weren't planted that way; that's how they had grown naturally.

If the fawn had gone through the front yard and across the dirt road that ran in front of the house, he should be fairly easy to find. The woods over there are somewhat sparse, with little underbrush. This would make the task of spotting Dandelion a simple one, or so I hoped. Beyond the woods was a field of grass where a shallow lake had once been. Enough years had not passed to produce the cover of trees or bushes. I doubted whether the fawn would venture into such an open area.

To the north of the house a short distance through the woods lay the 730-acre Lake Shishebogama. Between our house and the shore was a seventy-five-yard stretch of mostly oak woods. Beyond there, two log cottages overlooked the water. I doubted that Dandelion would have ventured near these dwellings. Searching the woods between wouldn't take that long.

I glanced at my watch: 6:03 P.M. exactly. I was halfway home. Suddenly a frightening thought crossed my mind. The highway I was traveling passed within 300 yards of my house. Given the fact that Dandelion had been hit by a car only two months before, I reassured myself—perhaps falsely—that the young deer must have learned his lesson. He wouldn't go back to the highway again, I hoped. If he did, it might already be too late.

The fawn's pen was located to the west, among the trees behind the house. I had strung a three-foot-high fence between the larger trees to form three sides of an enclosure that must have measured thirty by thirty feet. The fourth side of the pen was our house. I had suspected that this size was more than adequate for a small fawn with a broken leg. I was sure the designated area was adequate. However, even at this fawn's tender age, his instincts were already being manifested. Linda and I had observed that each night between five and six o'clock, Dandelion would become restless and fidgety. Like his wild counterparts, which have the urge to move about in early evening, Dandelion was driven by the same biological clock. This day his instincts carried him beyond the pen. He probably didn't even know why himself.

I thought the pen had all the amenities necessary for a growing fawn. The ground within was covered with several years' worth of fallen leaves. A few clumps of grass poked up here and there through the leafy floor. The rich green of the scattered ferns served as a constant reminder that it was summer in the north. They more or less hid the fence on two sides, making it difficult to discern that a pen was there at all. This should have given Dandelion a certain sense of privacy and freedom—maybe not enough, though.

In one corner I had broken several bales of straw to give Dandelion a comfortable place to rest. The straw was protected from wind and rain by an eight-foot plywood lean-to. The fawn somehow knew to go there whenever the weather threatened.

Besides the deluxe accommodations, Linda kept Dandelion literally stuffed with good food—alfalfa, clover, apples, and the like. Fresh water was provided constantly. Studies have proven conclusively that infant orphan mammals need touching stimulation to survive. This loving affection was supplied in generous amounts—compliments of my wife. Whenever we had a lull in the hospital action,

Linda would dash home to care for him. Dandelion should have been content, and I think he was. But he was driven by the forces that control all wild animals. He had to be free.

Behind the pen was the worst direction the fawn could have gone. Our property sloped downward back there— gradually at first, then more dramatically—into a huge, boggy area jammed with tamaracks and black spruce. Water stood year-round in lower spots, especially near uprooted pines that had fallen victim to windstorms. The spongy moss floor, with the water table close underneath, provided scant amounts of nutrition for the close-growing tamaracks—and even scanter support for their shallow roots. Each tree seemed to crowd into the next, making it difficult to distinguish the limbs of one from another. This gave the effect of a dark-green umbrella that dimmed the light in the bog on even the brightest of days. I was fascinated with bogs and had hiked the quarter-mile through this one on several occasions. Each time, I sensed an eeriness that was impossible to explain. It wasn't fear, for I had practically grown up in the woods of Michigan. Nonetheless, the bog had a spooky silence about it. The smothering pines, stagnant water, and spongy ground that sometimes jiggled under the step lent an almost sinister quality to the scene. I always felt relieved when my hike was completed. But for some reason, I was drawn back. The bogs weren't even a particularly good habitat for wildlife, so it would seem. Even birds were scarce down there.

As I sped home, I couldn't help but think of that forbidding place. I hoped Dandelion had not headed there.

The tires squealed as I turned sharply off the highway onto Minch Road. A short distance farther, I swung left and hurried the last quarter-mile to my driveway. I skidded to a halt just inches from the garage door. Linda was standing in the front yard, and I could tell by her look that her continuing search had not been successful.

Tears welled in her eyes and her voice cracked. "C'mon. We have to find him. I've already looked toward the highway and he's not there."

"We'll find him. . . . We'll find him," I reassured her. "You look down toward the lake and I'll look across the road."

"Okay," Linda choked and turned away toward the cottages.

I ran across the dirt road in front and into the woods. As I suspected, visibility was fairly good. Even though the camouflage markings would make Dandelion somewhat difficult to see, the tape and aluminum of the splint would serve as an aid to spot him. Quickly I canvassed back and forth. The orange of the impending sunset reflected off the trunks of the birch trees that were interspersed between the oak and occasional pine. No trace of him. I whirled around at a sudden noise behind me. A fat black squirrel was rooting under the leaves in search of last year's acorns. I startled him, and he scurried up a gnarly oak tree, where he sat on a low limb, chattering at my intrusion.

A bit farther and I was almost to the edge of the woodland meadow. The rat-tat-tat of an invisible woodpecker echoed from the hollow tree directly in front of me. I stopped in my tracks. My eyes scanned the dead tree to identify this Northwoods bird, providing a brief respite from my pressing search. In a few seconds, the busy fellow crept around to my side of the tree, hammering here and there at the bark. Except for his white back, the woodpecker's plumage was spotted and checkered in a symmetrical pattern with black and white. He sported a small red patch on his head, almost like a yarmulke. A hairy woodpecker, I thought. A Jewish woodpecker, I laughed to myself. The acrobatic bird spiraled around the tree and reappeared. No, it was a bit too small for a hairy, and the beak wasn't heavy enough.

"It's a downy," I whispered to myself. His noisy search for food stopped momentarily until I passed. I hadn't gone far when the dinnertime rat-tat-tat resumed, echoing through the trees.

I looked out across the grass where the small lake had been, perhaps a hundred years before. I jogged along the perimeter of the sawgrass, past a few lonely huckleberry bushes, confident that I would have been able to see some sign if Dandelion had ventured farther. I was quite sure that the fawn would not have left the cover of the trees, but I wanted to be positive. The dragging splint would have left telltale marks in the otherwise undisturbed grass. I skirted the edge but found no evidence of such a trail. Satisfied, I turned and headed back through the trees toward the house. Once on the higher ground, I stopped to listen and scrutinize the area. I stooped to pick from a wintergreen plant at my feet. I bit into the tender, aromatic leaf. Later on in the year the leaves would become hard, glossy, and leathery and not so tempting. But the ripe, red berries would be a delicacy. A hint of wintergreen filled the July air as I continued on.

As I neared the road, I spotted Linda returning from the lake. Since she was not carrying Dandelion, she obviously had not found him. We met in the front yard.

"No sign of him, huh?" I muttered, almost absent-mindedly.

Linda shook her head no but did not speak. She was completely out of breath. Her normally kempt appearance had yielded to the situation. A smudge mark streaked across her cheek. Her tanned face appeared flushed from the exercise. A pine needle was stuck in her tangled, dark-

brown hair above her left ear. I reached over and pulled the needle out and said what both of us had to be thinking. "He's in the bog area behind his pen."

My eyes met Linda's. A flash of hopelessness crossed her face. It was getting late in the day. I knew she was tormented. Linda looked upon her work with injured wildlings seriously, and fawns were her specialty.

"Listen," I told her, "regardless of what happens, it was not your fault. I'm the one who built the escape-proof pen."

"Yeah, but I'm the one who is taking care of him."

"Well, you can't keep your eye on him every second, Linda. Besides, we'll find him." I tried to comfort her.

"How in the world are we going to find him in the swamp?" Linda often referred to the bog area as "the swamp."

I didn't answer her at first. I was thinking. How would we cover the entire bog? Dandelion could be lost for a long time down there.

Just then, a bark from our year-old golden retriever, Tenille, interrupted our conversation.

"Tenille, that's Tenille," I remarked, my voice on the rise. "Where's Tenille?"

"She's in the house. When I noticed the fawn gone, I ran out so fast I forgot all about her." Linda could tell by my expression that I had an idea. Instantly, she knew what it was.

"Do you really suppose Tenille can help?" Linda stammered. I could see a glimmer of hope return to her blue eyes.

"I'm not sure, but it's worth a try." Golden retrievers

Black spruce are the dominant trees in this northwoods bog.

are not really tracking dogs, but they do have good noses. I knew, too, that Tenille and Dandelion were best buddies. They often played together for hours.

Linda and I bolted to the house to let our hoped-for bloodhound outside. Tenille barked and jumped up against the door before Linda could open it. Once outside, Tenille ran several circles around us, exploding with energy. Her coat was honey gold, a darker shade than most goldens. Her sleekness was enhanced by the long feathering on her tail.

"Linda, let's show Tenille something that has Dandelion's scent and then head out back. Do you have anything we can let her smell?" I knew that this was the procedure followed by handlers of search-and-rescue dogs. I wasn't sure it would work with an untrained golden looking for a deer, but it was all we had.

"I know what we can use," Linda stated and flew into the house. In a moment she reappeared with old bandage material that had been removed in the process of repairing the fawn's splint.

"This was in the wastebasket from when you retaped the splint last night." She held up a soiled wad of tape and gauze.

"Come, Tenille," Linda beckoned, as the three of us headed around back toward Dandelion's pen. Tenille immediately complied. The dog was trained in basic commands. Little did she know she was about to receive her first assignment in tracking.

Once behind the pen, Linda bent down and held the gauze and tape against Tenille's black nose. Tenille wagged her tail questioningly.

"Fetch Dandy. Fetch Dandy." Linda repeated the command we had taught Tenille and held the material against her nose again. The canine member of our search party was momentarily confused about what Linda wanted.

She stood waiting for Linda to throw the bandage. I hoped Tenille would understand that this "fetch" meant something different than she'd been taught.

"Fetch Dandy. Fetch Dandy." I could sense the desperation mounting in her voice. Tenille sensed this, too, and realized that this was not a game.

Linda again held the old bandage in front of the dog. "Fetch Dandy," she repeated and motioned outward with her arm.

Finally the command made sense to the dog. Tenille put her nose to the ground and began exploring the area. First this way and then that. "Fetch Dandy," Linda kept saying.

Tenille continued her rhythmic pattern, and with each pass she strayed farther and farther from us. As she neared the back of our property, she stopped abruptly. Through the ferns I could see her tail wagging furiously as she sniffed and nosed her way through the tangled underbrush, heading toward the bog.

"C'mon, Lin," I shouted and sprinted toward Tenille. "I think she's got his scent." Linda was right beside me in an instant. Even so, we were no match for the dog. By the time we reached the edge of the bog, Tenille was nowhere to be seen or heard.

For a time we stood and listened, unsure which way the dog had gone. A twig snapped somewhere off to our left, and I thought I heard a faint splashing sound.

"Listen, Lin." I pointed in the direction of the sounds. I thought I heard Tenille going through water. We stood silent. "There it is again," I said softly. "Let's go."

I grabbed Linda's hand, and we plunged forward. The boggy, wet ground shook under our combined weight. The going was relatively dry at first, but soon we were squishing through ankle-deep water and moss. The tamaracks overhead obscured the light. What light there was shimmered through the trees, producing a mottled pattern on the surface of the moss.

I pulled up short and tugged Linda's arm. "Let's listen again," I whispered. We stopped and listened intently. Tenille's faint whining could be heard deeper in the bog.

"Maybe she's found him!" I exclaimed. I tightened my grip on Linda's hand and lurched forward. I wasn't sure if Tenille had tracked down the fawn, but I didn't know why else she would whine.

We came to a dry spot again and climbed atop the decaying, moss-covered root system of a fallen tree. We still couldn't see the dog, but the whining was a bit louder now. We suddenly became aware of another familiar sound. It was the fawn bleating, a sound similar to that made by a lamb.

We caught our breath and strained forward, closing in on the uninterrupted whining and occasional bleating. The sounds became louder and louder—we were getting closer.

"Wait a minute," Linda yelled and tugged my arm hard. I turned to see her standing with one shoeless foot in the air.

"My heel wedged under a stick and my shoe pulled off." She was exasperated.

I stepped back a few feet, and reached down into the murky water where she pointed. In a moment I held up her drowned tennis shoe. Without untying it, she shoved it back on.

"C'mon, let's find Dandelion," she stammered. I marveled at my wife's perseverance.

Confident we were close, we pressed forward with renewed spirits. The sounds were coming from behind a fallen black spruce just up ahead. Tenille's tail flagged now and again above the trunk of the downed tree.

"Tenille, Tenille," Linda called. "Did you find Dandy?" Linda asked as if she expected an answer.

We approached rapidly now. Dandelion lay on a hummock, between two limbs of the spruce. The splint looked wet and dirty, but except for a bit of mud on the legs, the fawn looked remarkably clean. Dandelion wasn't in the least afraid of us, nor did he try to escape. In fact, his tail flicked several times as we neared. It looked as though he was glad to see us.

Tenille stood off to the side and wagged attentively. We stepped over the log, and I picked up Dandy. Together we examined the little patient.

"Except for needing a splint change, he's fine," I announced. Tears of joy and relief trickled down Linda's face. She bent down and wrapped her arms around Tenille's neck.

"You're the best dog in the whole world," she praised. For a time Linda sat, hugging our hero. "Good dog, good dog," Linda repeated many times. Tenille licked Linda's face, acknowledging the numerous accolades. She always received plenty of attention but never quite like this. "You're such a good dog, Neelie."

Still hugging Tenille, Linda looked up and spoke to the fawn.

"So you want to be free," she said. "We want that too, but not till your leg is healed. Do you think you can wait another six weeks?"

Linda turned again to the dog. "Thank you, thank you for saving Dandy." She stroked Tenille's head.

Dandelion settled in my arms, as though he anticipated the free ride he was about to receive. He nuzzled my hand as if looking for a snack.

Linda and I didn't talk much as we began our trek out of the bog. We were both exalted over the experience we had just shared. Nothing had to be said.

On my right, Tenille matched Linda's walk stride for stride. Our dog was more than just a beautiful golden and faithful companion. She was special.

We reached the edge of the bog, and up through the woods I could see the gold splashes of the setting sun on the side of our house. It was going to be dark in a short while. Out of the corner of my eye I saw Linda reach down and gently pat Tenille on the head.

"You're the best," she whispered.

The author's wife, Linda, hugs Tenille, now ten years old. Like all dogs, golden retrievers are faithful pets and good friends.

FOOD FOR THOUGHT

THE EARPIECES OF THE STETHOSCOPE FIRMLY IN PLACE, I bent down over the stainless-steel exam table to listen to Sammy's heartbeat. Sammy was a sixteen-week-old Sheltie owned by Margaret Jensen, an elderly woman of Finnish descent. She had told me once that her family in northern Wisconsin dated back 150 years, to the time her grandfather had settled just north of town and tried to farm the land. He found out the hard way what a lot of other folks in those days found out, too: the summers in the Northwoods, though comfortable, were simply too cold and too short to make a living from the land. Occasional clearings in the massive forest still serve as testaments to the gallant, though futile, efforts of the early settlers.

I could tell immediately upon placing the stethoscope on the side of Sammy's chest that something was wrong—drastically wrong. Instead of the rhythmic lub-dub, lub-dub, lub-dub, I could hear a sloshing sound that interfered with the normally clear and distinct heart sounds.

"Dr. Foster, I wasn't totally honest a minute ago when you asked me what I fed Sammy. I know that you recommend dog food only, but since he wasn't growing,

I've been giving him bacon and eggs in the morning to try and beef him up."

I wasn't sure why, but most clients liked to add an afterthought to their dog's history right when I was listening to the heart. I would have thought it would be obvious to most pet owners that it was very hard to hear their conversation while I had the stethoscope in place. Apparently it wasn't so obvious. Usually I simply ignored them until I finished this part of the exam, but Margaret was persistent.

"Bacon and eggs," she repeated. "I feed him bacon and eggs every morning."

I straightened up and removed the stethoscope.

"Bacon and eggs every day, huh?" I repeated back to her. "I wish I could afford to eat bacon every day," I said, half joking. Only half joking, because it was half true. I had started the practice less than one year before—just in time for a recession. The first year of any veterinary practice can be lean, but the economic situation had made things even worse. Of course, by most standards, I was still doing okay, but Linda and I still had to watch our budget. Bacon every day was a luxury we could not yet afford.

"Well, Dr. Foster, to tell you the truth, I don't buy bacon for myself every day either. But I had to try something to get this dog to grow."

I looked back at Sammy. Margaret was right about one thing: this dog was not growing at the normal rate. I reached down to stroke the dog's fur. His backbone was prominent to my touch, indicating poor condition. The fragile puppy also did not have the silky and glossy fur typical of his breed. Instead, Sammy's brown and white coat was rather dull and dry. Above his pointy nose, his eyes lacked the bright look I would have suspected in a vigorous, growing dog.

I replaced the stethoscope, hoping that Margaret was through talking, at least for a minute or two. The sloshing sound from the heart seemed louder than ever. The murmur was continuous—proof that blood was leaking constantly.

"Not many things can cause a murmur like this," I whispered to myself.

I listened again, paying particular attention to the exact area where the murmur sounded loudest. The intensity was most noticeable at the beginning of the second cardiac sound and seemed loudest at the left cardiac base. These findings confirmed what I was thinking.

I gently placed Sammy on the floor of the exam room and turned back to Margaret. "Now I know why your dog is not doing well. He has a heart defect called patent ductus arteriosis. We call it PDA for short."

I paused to study the owner. Margaret looked obviously distressed. Her tall, firm frame stiffened with the news. Her wrinkled knuckles, showing all her sixty-some-odd years, whitened as she clenched the leash she was holding. Her normally pleasant look vanished as she thought about what I just said.

"What exactly does this mean, Doctor? Is he going to die?"

I tried to be as matter-of-fact, yet as sympathetic as possible. I cleared my throat and began.

"I don't think Sammy is going to die. In fact, he could live a normal life, but"—I paused again—"he will need surgery. You see, patients with a PDA have an abnormal channel that allows blood to cross over from the left side of the heart to the right. By doing so, the blood bypasses the lungs, eventually affecting the entire body. That's why Sammy is not growing as he should."

I glanced down at the dog and then back to Margaret. Her gray hair looked almost white under the fluorescent light of the room.

"You mean I won't have to buy bacon and eggs for him in the future? Just dog food will do?" she said and smiled.

I like people who have a sense of humor under fire. Margaret's comment lightened up the atmosphere, making it easier to discuss the specifics of Sammy's surgery.

"'Doc, the dog means the world to me. He's all I have now." Margaret hesitated, then proceeded. "As you no doubt know, my husband passed away last year and Sammy and I live alone, but I do have to ask what all this is going to cost."

There it was—the inevitable question. That was one thing I hated about veterinary medicine. The care for any particular dog or cat depended on the owner's ability and willingness to pay. Margaret didn't know it, but my hospital policy was that no animal would be put to sleep because of an owner's inability to pay the bill. Of course, I didn't advertise that fact.

Minocqua is a small town; therefore I had known about Margaret's husband before she told me. I felt sorry for the old woman. I suspected she wasn't financially very well off. Not that someone's car is always the gauge, but I had seen her driving around town in a white Valiant that had to be at least ten years old.

"Well, Margaret, for everything—surgery, anesthetic, and hospitalization—the fee would be about one hundred twenty-five dollars." I knew that for the type of surgery this was a very low quote, but I wanted to keep it within her means. Besides, I wanted to do it.

"A hundred and twenty-five dollars? That's all?" She sounded surprised and relieved. "I would've thought heart surgery would be a lot more. Are you sure you're charging enough, Dr. Foster?"

"Sure, that's enough. We call it heart surgery, but the surgery is really next to the heart, not right in it. Besides, it will be a learning experience for me." Because this type of surgery was uncommon in private practice, I really did want to do it. But her remarks left me with a sense of vulnerability. Maybe I should have charged her what the surgery was worth—three or four hundred dollars. After all, I'd learn as much either way. Of course, maybe my initial thought was correct. This woman reallly didn't have much money. I knew she didn't.

Margaret left her dog, and later that day I telephoned Dr. T. J. Dunn who, in my opinion, was the best veterinary surgeon in the area. Whenever I was faced with a two-person surgery, I relied on T.J. for help. Besides, I had worked for him for a time after graduation, so the two of us were good friends.

T.J. arrived right on schedule at seven-thirty that evening. Because of the quiet phone, I often planned lengthy or complicated procedures at night. This also meant I could count on Linda's uninterrupted help.

Midway through the surgery, during a lull in the conversation, a screech reverberated from the kennel and into the surgery room.

T.J. looked nervously at Linda, who was monitoring the anesthetic and then shot a sideways glance across the table at me.

Neither Linda nor I acknowledged T.J.'s concern. We knew what the noise was.

"All right, you guys, what was that weird noise?" T.J. demanded. "You told me that you were starting to treat a few wild animals now and then. That noise certainly did not come from a dog or cat. What do you have back there, anyway?"

T.J. was correct. I did have an interest in treating injured wild creatures. Linda and I had a fawn at home that we were nursing back to health, and I had a goshawk and a great horned owl in the hospital kennel. Both birds had been hit by cars and had sustained broken wings.

Until the bones healed, each would be staying in the hospital. This would mean at least another month in the vet clinic.

I looked over at T.J. as he bent over the patient. The glare of the surgery lights reflected off his prematurely balding head. After all, he was only thirty-two.

I laughed aloud and so did Linda. Again, we heard from the kennel.

"You're right," Linda replied. "That noise is not from a dog or cat. It sounds as if either Talon or Shakespeare is hungry."

It was hard to see T.J.'s expression under his surgery mask, but his eyes and brow looked perplexed.

"Who are Talon and Shakespeare?"

"Feathered patients of ours," Linda answered. "Rory fixed their wings. We want to let them go as soon as they have healed." I could hear the excitement building in Linda's voice. She got as much enjoyment out of helping injured wildlife as I did. In fact, she was completely in charge of taking care of the fawn at home.

"Talon is a hawk, and Shakespeare is the owl," Linda beamed. "Neither is long on patience when they want to eat."

It was evident that T.J.'s curiosity was aroused now.

"What in the world do you feed them anyway?" T.J. asked.

With that question Linda wrinkled her nose. I could tell the subject was distasteful for her so I entered the conversation.

"Well, to tell you the truth, T.J., that's one of the major problems I've encountered dealing with wild patients. It's hard to find suitable food. Birds of prey like the ones I have back there can exist for short periods on meat scraps supplemented with vitamins and minerals. But best results are seen by duplicating their natural diet."

T.J. looked up from the surgery. I could tell by his expression that he was not at all certain he wanted to hear more.

"How do you duplicate a natural diet of a hawk or owl?" The words came out hesitantly.

"About the closest I can come is to pick up road-killed animals when I find them. You know, rabbits and stuff like that. Actually they're pretty easy to find in the summer, but I have to admit, it's not one of my favorite tasks."

"Well, if I find anything you could use on my next trip up, I'll stop and pick it up for you."

That sounded good to me. I really didn't have time to scrounge the local highways anyway. I could use any help.

About ten minutes later, the patent ductus next to Sammy's beating heart was isolated. Together we placed two heavy ligatures around the ductus. By tightening the ligatures, we accomplished for Sammy what his body should have done at birth. The abnormal channel was closed, and circulation throughout the heart area became normal. With a little luck Sammy would enjoy a full life.

Sammy went home three days later, and it was already obvious that he was improving. By the time I saw him for suture removal one week after discharge, he had already gained three pounds. Needless to say, Margaret Jensen was pleased.

I didn't see Margaret or Sammy again for about three weeks, until our unexpected meeting. I had left for work

Injured hawks are common patients at the author's hospital. This red-tail was investigating a road-killed rabbit when it was struck by an automobile.

about five-thirty that morning to give myself time to drive around a bit in search for road-kills for Talon, Shakespeare, and two additional owls that were patients of mine. When I spotted what appeared to be a freshly killed rabbit on the highway, I quickly edged my Bronco onto the shoulder and got out with a brown paper grocery bag. I had just picked up the rabbit and was about to place it in the sack when a car pulled up behind me.

In the early morning light I recognized Sammy sitting in the front seat of a new white Cadillac. His noseprints adorned the partially rolled down window on his side. The driver's door opened, and with hardly a word of greeting, the driver strolled directly over to me. For an instant she stood there staring at the hapless rabbit dangling from my hand.

"I told you that you should charge more," Margaret suddenly said. With that she shoved a fifty-dollar bill in my back pocket. "Here," she ordered, "go buy yourself some good food."

FRAN AND MAGGIE

FRANCES LOUISE DELTON AND MARGARET LEONA WEBB BURST through the front door of the clinic.

"Get Rory, get Rory," Fran demanded of Linda. "Hurry, honey, where's Rory?" Her voice sounded raspy. Her asthma always acted up in summer. The pack of cigarettes she smoked daily didn't help either.

Linda looked up and over the pale-yellow reception counter at Fran and Maggie.

"Don't just stand there," Fran ordered. "Get the doctor." Fran was practically out of breath.

It was 1:00 P.M.—nearly an hour before our first afternoon appointment; there were no clients in the hospital. Linda ignored the usual office protocol and simply yelled for me.

"Ror, Ror, come to the front." Linda's firm but feminine voice reached back to the prep room where I was just finishing cleaning a setter's teeth. I disconnected the endotracheal tube from the gas anesthetic machine and placed the dog on a white blanket in the recovery cage.

"Just a second," I hollered back. "I have to be sure

this dog is okay." I rubbed the elderly setter's sleek mahogany side to wake up the patient.

My lack of punctuality was more than Fran could handle. The solid oak door connecting the front reception area to the back of the clinic banged open against the wall.

"Come on, Doc," Fran bellowed. "We have an eagle that needs you. You said you liked working on wildlife, so here's your chance."

I stuck my head out of the cage and looked at Fran. The retired army nurse stood a few feet away, one hand on her hip. Her car keys jangled nervously in the other hand. Even through her sunglasses, I could see the spunk in her eye. Her curt haircut and prominent cheekbones accented her imposingly large, stout figure—hidden within her baggy clothes. Her navy blue nylon windbreaker was unzipped. A toothpick danced back and forth across her lower lip. She must have been a good nurse, I thought.

"What do you mean you have an eagle?" I questioned. "Where?"

Maggie's white hair and round, grandmotherly face poked through the door. "We just saw him—" Maggie started to explain.

"He's just off Highway Fifty-one by Airport Road," Fran cut Maggie off. Fran had a habit of doing most of the talking. Perhaps her authoritative manner was a hold-over from her rank as major in the Korean War. Maggie's quiet, unassuming personality allowed Fran to dominate; at least that's the way it looked.

The setter swallowed. He was finally waking up. I gently pulled the trach tube from his throat. I closed the door of the steel cage and stood up.

"An eagle by Airport Road." I paused and removed my lab coat. "Is he injured?"

"That's for you to find out, honey," Fran emphasized. "Maybe it fell out of its nest during this morning's rainstorm. You know, we have a nest on our road. Maggie and I pass it every day on the way to town. It's only about two miles from the kennel."

I had heard about the eagle's nest north of town, but was not exactly sure where it was.

"Well, let's go take a look." I turned to Linda, who had been listening intently. "Airport Road isn't that far from here, so I shouldn't be long." I followed Fran and Maggie out to the parking lot.

"Follow us," Fran yelled to me over her shoulder. "Hurry up, Maggie. We don't have all day," I heard her say. Fran was constantly badgering Maggie, but the chiding always seemed to be good-natured. This was evidenced by Maggie's benign perpetual smile. She took it all in stride, or so it seemed.

I jumped in my Bronco and followed their red and white jeep truck out of the parking lot. Small bits of sand and rock bounced against my windshield from their tires. I slacked off the gas and dropped farther behind.

Once on the highway, I sped up, determined not to lose sight of their jeep. Fran and Maggie—I laughed to myself. What characters! They stopped by the clinic nearly every day to visit Linda and me. I told them what was going on at the hospital, and they told me what was going on in town. They somehow always knew the latest.

The two ladies lived in a duplex several miles out of town across from the area's small airport. They owned and operated an adjoining boarding kennel. Besides boarding, they also provided safe haven for the area's stray and abandoned dogs, almost like the humane shelters in cities. Some of the surrounding townships paid them a token amount for their efforts, but it was never enough to cover even the minimal expenses of food and shelter. Fran and Maggie weren't involved with the strays for the money. They were genuinely caring people.

Of course, Fran occupied a special place in my heart

for another reason, a reason I tried to forget. The year before, her chocolate-brown toy poodle, Bumper, had been the first surgery patient in my new hospital.

Fran had brought Bumper in for a recurring problem with his anal sacs. The dog's scent glands, located next to the anus, were always bothering him. Historically, Bumper's ancestors may have had use for the glands, but in modern-day dogs the glands serve no discernible purpose. As is customary in veterinary medicine for chronic anal sac problems, I offered to remove them.

Surgery consists of splitting the muscles surrounding the anus and dissecting through the tissue in order to remove the two grape-sized glands. Once they have been removed, the incision is simply sewn back up, and the dog heals without incident. At least, that's what's supposed to happen. Bumper had to be different. Maybe my dissection had bruised too many muscles or nerves. Something happened.

Two days after I sent Bumper home, Fran called. She was frantic.

"Is the rectum supposed to look like this?" she asked.

"Look like what?"

"Well, something is sticking out of his little hinder. It's about two inches long and looks like a red, angry mass. It must be a prolapsed rectum, Doc. If I push it back in, it comes out if he barks."

Damn, damn, damn, I muttered to myself. My first surgery patient in my brand-new hospital and I blew it. Plus, Fran knew everyone in town. Why did *she* have to own the dog?

Above: Margaret Webb on patrol to keep the kennel grounds clean. Below: Frances Delton leans against the truck that bears her kennel's name.

"You'd better bring Bumper in." I regained my composure. "Let me take another look."

Fran brought Bumper in right away. Sure enough, the surgery had somehow traumatized the muscles around the anus, causing the opening to be quite flaccid. He could not control his rectal muscles. Thankfully the dog was not in pain.

The whole mess still gives me a hollow feeling. I ended up having to do a major procedure called a colopexy to tack the large intestine to the abdominal wall, thereby preventing any future prolapses. The dog healed fine after that, but I'm sure that little poodle took ten good years off my life.

Fran never blamed me, and I'm still not certain if surgical error caused the complication. Maybe it would have happened anyway. Since then we had become the best of friends, and Linda and I looked forward to Fran and Maggie's frequent visits. During these conversations Fran never mentioned Bumper and the problems we had. Had she forgotten?

Fran swerved in front of me to pass a car. She seemed to be able to handle the car well, but definitely was driving too fast. Fran had told me once that she had some experience driving semis. I had doubted it before, but not now.

The flashing left blinker and brake lights of the jeep indicated that we were about to turn. Oncoming traffic prevented an immediate turn and allowed me to pull up right behind the two women. Once onto Airport Road, Fran drove slowly, hunched over the steering wheel and peering to the right for the eagle.

We had gone barely a tenth of a mile when I could see Maggie pointing out her window. The jeep slammed to a halt causing the two heads to lurch forward. I laughed aloud and pulled off the road behind them. I grabbed Tenille's tattered red blanket in case I needed it.

I could see the eagle from the road. It stood behind a small jack pine between a weathered gray fence post and a larger pine. The bird looked nearly three feet tall as it stood eyeing us suspiciously. Its brown feathers were completely drenched, evidence of the earlier downpour. Only the dusky-colored head appeared to be dry.

"Sure is big for a youngster," Maggie offered. "How old do you think this bird is, anyway?"

"Eagles are born sometime in May but grow remarkably fast. They're nearly full size after only a couple of months." I looked from Maggie to the eagle. Its presence was truly commanding.

"What do we do now, Doc?" Fran asked.

I thought for a moment. I wasn't an eagle expert by any means. "Obviously this eagle has fallen from its nest." I had seen the nest from the road. It was about seventy-five yards deeper in the woods in a mammoth dead pine. We talked quietly and walked toward the eagle.

"I guess the only way we'll know if this one is hurt is to take him back to the hospital," I muttered, not totally confident of the situation. "If I can catch him, I'll put him in the cardboard box in the back of my Bronco. He'll be safe there for transport."

Maggie offered to get the box and turned back toward the vehicles a short distance away.

Cautiously I approached the eagle. I knew from past experience with raptors that the feet could be dangerous. If only I'd brought my leather glove.

On my request, Fran circled behind the eagle to prevent him from hopping farther into the woods. I approached from the front and was surprised when he did not try to escape.

When I was within about ten feet, the eagle sprang to action. His yellowish-brown bill opened, and he hissed several times. His tall size and open beak gave him a fierce look that alarmed even Fran.

"Look out for his beak, Doc," Fran warned. "He looks mighty mean."

"Don't worry. Eagles don't use their beaks that much for defense. It's the feet I'm worried about."

I inched closer. The massive wings started to spread. I stopped, and the wings returned to their resting place against his body. My immediate concern were his weapons—powerful yellow legs and menacing razorlike talons. I inched still closer.

With both hands, I opened the blanket. If I can throw it over him, I thought, I can grab the legs. I cursed myself again for having forgotten my protective glove.

My sudden leap forward startled Fran and the bird. They squawked simultaneously, a fact that Fran later denied. I threw the red quilt over the eagle and in one motion grabbed both legs with my left hand. He struggled at first, but the leghold rendered him virtually helpless. The blanket removed, I cradled him on his back, much as one would carry a baby, my right arm wrapped around his body to prevent his brawny wings from flailing. I rotated his body slightly away from mine to prevent bites.

Fran and I turned to Maggie, who had silently witnessed the spectacle. "Get over here with the box," Fran barked.

Maggie complied and ambled forward, enamored with the bird. "Jeez, is he pretty! Look at those eyes," Maggie marveled.

"Put the box down. We'll hold it open so Rory can put the bird in it," Fran said to Maggie.

Maggie placed the cardboard box on the ground beside me. Gingerly, I placed the patient inside and closed the flaps. The eagle fumbled for a second, then found secure footing. In the darkness of the box, he quieted down immediately.

I placed the box in the back of the Bronco and prepared to return to the clinic.

"Are you coming with me?" I invited Fran and Maggie. "Why don't you two come with me to examine the eagle?"

Fran looked down at her watch. "It's after two already, and we have three boarders going home this afternoon. We'll have to head back to the kennel. Give us a call, though, honey, and let us know what's wrong."

"All right, will do," I replied. "I'll call you as soon as I know something."

Linda heard me pull into my usual parking spot in front of the clinic. She held the doors open so I could carry the box inside. A springer spaniel tugged tenaciously at a leather leash. At the other end, seated on the oak bench in the reception room, his owner peeked curiously over the recent issue of *People* magazine he had been reading.

"Sorry I'm a little late," I called to him. "I'll be with you in a flash." Linda and I headed back to the prep room. The door swung closed behind us.

"What's in there? What've you got in the box?" Linda could not contain her excitement.

"Shhh. Try to be as quiet as you can. There's a bald eagle in here!" I whispered. We were both excited. Our wildlife treatment program was in its infancy, and we were still not used to the spectacular patients, especially ones like this.

For the time being, I set the box on the floor in the corner. "Don't open the box now," I said to Linda. "We'll examine the bird later, when we get a break in our appointments. Don't worry, he's not bleeding or anything like that."

Linda kindly ushered the gentleman and his springer into the first exam room. Routine vaccines. Fortunately, the next four appointments were vaccinations also. Finally, at 3:30, Linda announced that we had nothing scheduled for an hour. It was the eagle's turn.

I started to open the box when the phone rang. "Darn

it," I said to Linda. "If we're going to get time to examine the eagle, we can't be interrupted. Once I get him out of the box, we can't keep putting him back. It's too much handling." The phone rang again. "After that call, Lin, take the phones off the hook."

Linda answered. "Hi, Fran," I heard her say. "We're just looking right now." There was a pause. "Yes, I know. Rory has been back for over an hour. He had appointments."

"Linda, tell her we'll call her in thirty minutes, promise," I interjected.

Fran must have agreed to wait for our call. Linda hung up the phone and then took it off the hook.

I finished opening the box. Wearing a leather glove, I reached down and once again grabbed the eagle's legs.

"He's huge!" Linda exclaimed. Her eyes widened in disbelief. "I can't believe how big he is."

He looked even larger to me than he had in the woods. Maybe he grew on the way here, I mused.

Of course, he hadn't really grown, but in the confines of the hospital his regal presence seemed to fill the room. I held him securely while Linda stretched first one wing and then the other. The eagle's heavy panting belied his otherwise calm demeanor.

Except for being soaked with water, the wings and flight feathers appeared intact. I could palpate no fractures.

Both eyes were symmetrical, a good sign that there was no eye damage or head trauma. Both legs appeared normal as far up as I could feel. I visually examined his toes. All okay.

"I'd bet anything, Lin, that this eagle was blown out of the nest during the rainstorm and fell to the ground. He probably would have been able to fly if it weren't for the drenched feathers. He undoubtedly flapped his wings enough to cushion the fall. That's why he's not injured.

More likely, he's just cold, wet, and hungry. We'd better take an X ray just to be certain that there are no broken bones or dislocations." I'd seen other large birds that had fallen from high nests under similar conditions. Sometimes there were injuries that could not be detected except by X ray.

I carried the eagle into the X ray room and held him while Linda readied the machine. Obtaining a readable radiograph on birds is always a little tricky—a little treacherous. It's difficult to hold them still, yet keep the hands out of the exposure field.

Fortunately this young eagle was in a cooperative mood. I held on to the dangerous feet and laid him on his back on the table. When I had positioned him exactly where I wanted him, I stepped on the foot pedal. The machine whirred and then clicked. The eagle had not moved.

The X ray taken, I put the majestic patient into a cement dog run. This afforded him a considerable amount of room and had good air exchange, which would facilitate rapid drying of his plumage. Linda procured a small log from outside, and I pushed it toward him where he stood in the back of the run. He glared at us for a moment and then hopped aboard his makeshift perch.

I developed the X rays and read them. No problems.

"Fran, it's me," I said when she answered her phone. "Good news. I can't find any evidence of serious injury. I think the eagle just got very wet up in the nest and couldn't fly. I'll keep him overnight to dry him out and give him a good meal or two; then let's take him back tomorrow. I'm sure he'll be fine." Suddenly it dawned on me that I'd been referring to the eagle as "him" when actually there is no easy way to tell the eagle sexes apart. Even at four to five years of age when this eagle would don a white head and tail, determining its sex would still be impossible for the onlooker.

"Oh, good. Does that mean we get to go with you, Doc?" Fran coaxed. "Just tell us the time, honey, and we'll meet you where we found him."

"Sounds okay to me, Fran. How about eight-thirty tomorrow morning before my appointments start? I'll meet you on Airport Road."

"Okay, honey. Maggie and I'll be there. Good. See you in the A.M. Bye, Rory."

"Good-bye."

After the remainder of the day's appointments, I drove to a nearby bait shop to purchase dinner for our friend. Before we left for the day, the eagle heartily ate seven whole shiners.

I returned alone at about 10:00 P.M. to give our overnight guest a bedtime snack. He gulped down two more shiners. I was amazed at how readily this bird ate in captivity. By this time his feathers were completely dry. He'd be ready to be released by morning. I turned out the light and went home.

Linda and I headed east from our house near Shish. It was seven-fifteen in the morning. I'd have time enough to do the morning treatments and still meet Fran and Maggie at the designated time and place.

"Look!" Linda pointed out the window. "There's a fawn!"

I looked over to see a doe and her spindly, spotted fawn gracefully disappear into the green wilderness just beyond the Tomahawk River.

"I just love it up here," Linda sighed. "Down in Florida I never saw animals like this. We see deer practically every day, and now we even have an eagle in the clinic. How many other people are so lucky?"

"Of course, how much wildlife was there in Fort Lauderdale where you lived?" I teased. Linda had actually grown up in a suburb of Milwaukee but moved to south

Florida when she was a senior in high school. She had spent the next eight years or so in Lauderdale.

We had met two years ago in Rhinelander, a town twenty-five miles southeast of Minocqua. That's where I started working after graduation from vet school. Linda was visiting her sister, Carole. Linda's Lhasa, Buffy, was injured, and T. J. Dunn and I were her vets. Of course, there's an unwritten code of ethics in the medical profession that doctors do not date patients. I applaud that code and swore in college I'd never date a patient—but the owner of the patient, that's something quite different. I was not so honorable. Linda and I married less than a year after Buffy's injury brought us together.

We turned off the highway and then into the gravel parking lot of the Foster Animal Hospital. Once inside the clinic we immediately checked the eagle. He was fine and even a bit noisy. He handily ate a few more plump minnows.

"I can't get over how gorgeous he is," Linda remarked. "How long do they live, anyway?" she inquired as I wrestled him out of the run and into the box.

"Believe it or not, eagles can live to be fifty years old. Hopefully, this one has forty-nine and three quarters left." I placed the feathered patient in the box and taped the top shut. "There, that ought to hold you for a few minutes till you get home."

In the darkness of his temporary shelter, the eagle rode quietly along with me to meet Fran and Maggie. I arrived at our rendezvous point at eight-fifteen. The two women were waiting.

"Hi, Doc. How's Lockheed?" Fran greeted.

"Lockheed? Who's Lockheed?" After I asked, I realized that she and Maggie must have named the eagle. They were quick to name every stray dog brought to them. This practice of naming critters continued. I should have known.

"Just great. Lockheed's just great. I bet he's anxious to get back in the woods, too. Of course, he got a free meal or two, so he shouldn't complain too much."

"What did you feed him, if I may ask?" Maggie was always polite.

"I gave him fish. That's what eagles usually eat in the wild," I told her.

"Let's go. We haven't got all day, guys. The Reddingtons are dropping off their labs at nine. We've got to be there for them," Fran reminded. "Besides, Lockheed probably doesn't like that box."

I carried the box, and Fran and Maggie followed me into the woods in the direction of the nest. I didn't want to get too close to the nest tree, but neither did I want to leave the bird within sight of the road. There were a couple of eagle shootings every year in the Northwoods. I was taking no chances.

We entered a small clearing about one hundred feet from the old dead tree. A parent eagle sat watching attentively from the lookout point above the lofty nest of sticks. I gazed upward. The nest had to be at least ten feet across.

Carefully, I untaped the box. I turned it sideways, and the eagle hopped out. In an instant he climbed, limb by limb, halfway up a nearby white pine, testing his wings as he jumped upward.

"There's no doubt in my mind. This eagle is fine," I reassured Fran and Maggie.

A series of shrieks rang out from the sentinel above. The mother was calling to the youngster.

"Let's get out of here. We can't do any more." I turned and started toward the road.

Fran and Maggie followed me out single file back to the trucks. I got into my Bronco. Before the two other members of the wildlife rescue team could settle into their jeep, I drove around them and turned around.

As I neared their jeep again, I slowed and rolled my window down for a few parting shots. I started to thank them when Fran interrupted.

"You didn't do any surgery on Lockheed's hinder, did you?" Fran quipped and burst into laughter.

Before I could gather my wits and reply, Fran waved and spun away.

HUNDREDS OF
ANIMALS—ACRES
OF FUN

IT WASN'T LONG AFTER I STARTED TREATING INJURED WILD-life and releasing them back to their natural habitats that the local newspaper, the *Lakeland Times*, picked up on the story. Soon I was receiving phone calls from interested persons all over the Midwest. Some were vets who wanted nothing more than to lend encouragement. Still others wanted to become members of the nonprofit organization so as to help with the eventual construction of the planned wildlife hospital.

There were other calls as well. One came from Orville's Wild Animal Roundup, a roadside wildlife exhibit several counties west of Minocqua.

"Hullo, this is Orville Dobson, over here at the wild-animal farm. You know, west of you on Seventy. About an hour away."

"Yeah, I think I know where you are." I had seen Orville's advertisements in the newspaper. His ads ran weekly all summer long to attract tourists to the Roundup. Apparently he had quite a menagerie of animals to see.

"Well, Doc, I read your article in the paper. Doc Barnes has been our vet for years, but he's been threatening to retire. If he does, would you like a shot at it?

Sounds like you're into wildlife." Orville reminded me of a used-car salesman.

"What do you mean exactly? I'm kind of far away for you to bring animals here to my hospital." I tried not to be too encouraging. My interest was in treating animals that live in the wild—not in captivity.

"No, Doc, what I mean is for you to come here. You know, maybe once a month in the spring and summer. That's what Doc Barnes does. For rabies vaccines and once in a while something else."

I hesitated. "Well, I don't know. It's kind of hard to get away, especially during the summer, but why don't you let me think about it and get back to you in a few days." I didn't have any experience with wildlife exhibits like Orville's, but several clients had described questionable conditions at similar businesses closer to home. Before I got involved, I wanted to see firsthand, to make up my own mind.

"You could work whatever hours you wanted—evenings, weekends, we don't care." Orville coaxed.

"It sounds like a pretty good offer." I thought for a moment. "But I'll tell you what. Give me a few more days and I'll call you." I did like working with wild animals, and Orville's place would give me experience. Maybe it wasn't such a bad idea. I'd check it out.

On Sunday, four days after Orville and I had talked, Linda and I decided to make an anonymous inspection of the Roundup. Other than my picture in the newspaper, Orville had never seen me. I had shaved my beard after the photo was taken, so I doubted I would be recognized. There was something about an incognito visit that intrigued us. We were on a spy mission.

Dust hovered over the busy gravel parking lot. Small signs that read "To the Animals" were strategically placed along the trail to the entrance. They were cut in the shape of a human hand with a finger pointing to the main gate.

A green and yellow arch towered over the ticket booth. I read out loud the bold block letters emblazoned overhead: "HUNDREDS OF ANIMALS—ACRES OF FUN."

"Where did you read that?" Linda looked at me. A hint of perspiration covered her forehead and cheeks. It was going to be hot.

"Up there." I pointed.

Linda looked at the arch and nodded. We paid our $3.50 each and entered through the turnstile. A large white sign in the configuration of an upright polar bear greeted us: "Welcome. The wild animals are on display for your entertainment and education. Enjoy." Signed, "Orville." Below the man's name was a map of the grounds.

Linda and I studied the map.

"What do you want to see first?" I asked. I glanced at my wife.

"Ror, did that boy just throw a frog in the water?" Linda was looking in the direction of a stagnant pond behind the sign.

"I don't know. I didn't see it." I peered around the sign. "Let's go see."

Linda and I walked the short distance to the pool. A small, freckle-faced boy stood on the shoreline cheering wildly. As we approached, he drew back and tossed again. Splat. The frog hit the water and kicked rhythmically toward shore.

Whoosh. An unexpected ferocious swirling of the water surprised both of us. The ripples calmed. The frog was gone. The boy clapped gleefully and jumped up and down on the bank.

"Mommy, could I buy some more frogs?" The youngster yelled to a woman sitting on a bench alongside a nearby concession stand.

"What's going on?" Linda was curious.

I read the sign above the stand: "Muskie and otter

feed—Frogs: 50 cents, Minnows: 26 cents." That's all I had to read.

"Linda, you're not going to believe this, but they're selling frogs to throw to the fish. You know, the muskies." I searched Linda's face.

"You're kidding!" Linda was distraught.

"I'm not." I pointed to the concession stand. There was something unsettling about this. It wrenched the senses. Of course, I knew that muskies sometimes ate frogs, but to make a sport and spectacle out of the frogs' plight was repulsive. Further, the fact that the young lad willfully caused and then delighted in the frog's demise gnawed at my gut. The frog's death should not have been mere amusement.

I gripped Linda's hand. "Come on. Let's keep going."

The closest cages contained the wild cats. A lone and lonely bobcat crouched on a log that leaned against the side of his cage. His tawny coat was matted and dull. A silver dollar–sized sore on his right hip glistened in the sun. It was covered with a pale-yellow ointment—probably prescsribed by ol' Doc Barnes, I thought. Whenever a fly would land near the lesion, the bobcat would jerk his head backward to scare off the pest.

Next door, a cougar paced around and around the perimeter of his circular enclosure. Our presence did not interrupt his purposeful maneuvers. He panted heavily in the heat. His pink tongue rolled out of his open mouth now and again. Drips of frothy saliva spatted on the cement.

A male lion rested in the shade in the next exhibit. Except for an occasional twitching of his long tail, he never moved. A chipmunk scurried from one side of the lion's cage to the big cat's feed dish, then back again. Apparently the lion did not mind sharing his lunch.

"You know, I've never liked zoos," Linda volunteered.

"Neither have I."

A patch of grass separated the cats from the next animal. The sign read: "Capybara, World's Largest Rodent." The creature was endowed with a compact, dense body, almost piglike. His sawed-off square snout gave his head the appearance of a cross between a beaver and hippo. Despite the passersby the capybara continued to snooze.

Laughter and shouts emanated from people surrounding a group of small cages under a canopylike roof. We headed in that direction.

The words "Pet Me Zoo" appeared in red lettering on a white cloth banner stretched at head level across one end. There was one attendant attempting to supervise some twenty-odd children and the animals. Two boys passed a large white rabbit back and forth as if amazed at his size.

"Can you believe how much he weighs?" I heard one of them say. He held the rabbit around the midsection. It struggled a bit and tried to claw with its hind feet.

"That's not the right way to handle him," I said to the blond kid holding the rabbit. "The best way is to grab a handful of loose skin over the shoulders and put your other hand under his back feet. Like this." I took the rabbit from him.

Both boys stared at me for a second, then walked away. Obviously they weren't really that interested. I started to place the rabbit back in his cage.

"Here, I'll do that," a female voice stopped me. I hesitated, and the attendant snatched the rabbit. She grasped the animal around its middle and tossed him into the cage.

I walked up behind Linda, who was watching three boys roughhouse with a coyote pup. One boy held the muzzle closed until the infant coyote cried loud enough to attract attention. He finally let go.

Kids of all ages ogled, petted, patted, stroked, cuddled, and fondled the baby skunks, ferrets, racoons, squirrels, and hamsters. Calico kittens and black, furry puppies scurried underfoot. Lambs, goat kids, and geese begged for handouts.

Around the corner from the petting zoo was Uncle Zeb's Chicken Coop. Bright yellow and red devices lined one wall of the "coop." We walked closer. Each circuslike machine contained a "trained" animal. For a quarter, a bantam chicken would dance around in his cubicle. Put a quarter in the slot in the machine next door and a large "educated" rooster would peck the appropriate lever in order to receive a ration of corn. Past the chickens, a rabbit huddled in the corner of his glass box. For fifty cents, he would "kiss" the front of his cage. Rabbit pellets would then roll down the chute. Linda and I spent no money.

The screaming whine of go-cart engines grew louder as we walked toward the wolves. A ten-foot-high wooden fence acted as a visual barrier between Orville's go-cart track and three identical cages. The first cage was labeled "Gray Wolf," the second "Timber Wolf," and the third "Arctic Wolf." Each time the go-carts whizzed behind the fence, the wolf designated "timber wolf" would tuck his tail and momentarily hunker down. A smoky blue haze filtered between the slats and over the fence. The smell of gasoline and fuel oil lingered in the air.

"Lin, by looking at the signs you'd think there were three different species here." I nudged my wife. "Don't these people know that all three are timber wolves—just different colors?"

To the left and back toward the entrance were the bears. An adult black bear sat attentively behind a sign that read: "Feed Pop Here."

"Linda, does that sign mean we're supposed to buy a bottle of soda and stick it through there? Or does that

THE EDUCATED HEN

Watch her perform   Receive a Gift

Above: An imprisoned timber wolf takes a break from his endless pacing. Facing page: For a quarter, this chicken will "perform."

mean the bear's name is Pop? Or if you really don't like your father, do you stick him through here?" I couldn't stop laughing.

The joke eased the building tension. Neither of us was impressed with Orville's Wild Animal Roundup. As I suspected, this place was similar to or worse than the many others that littered Wisconsin.

This roadside zoo was nothing more than a tourist attraction. Animals were exploited in the worst possible way. If there was an educational value, it eluded me. Rather, this mistreatment of animals might, in fact, teach that such cruelty is acceptable.

Roadside zoos are not at all like real zoos—which I don't particularly like either. I never like to see animals permanently confined. But at least real zoos are run by professionals for scientific or truly educational purposes; roadside zoos are run solely for profit.

The limited budgets of the RZs, as I call them, restrict the type of care that can be provided. Very often, as with Orville's, wild animals are kept in cages that are too small or otherwise unsuitable. In many cases, animals are kept singly, never to be in contact with others of their species. Even clean cages do not alter the inherent cruelty of keeping a lone wolf or bear in a small cage.

Like most roadside zoos, the Roundup thrives during the tourist season. Public support of RZs stems from a lack of understanding. Uninformed or unwitting individuals patronize such places and keep them in business.

In a roadside zoo, a Wisconsin black bear waits for a treat. The author thinks that roadside zoos exploit animals. Visitors to such places perpetuate the tragedy.

This kind of substandard zoo is not confined to private roadside enterprises. Municipalities, too, very often keep a variety of wild animals on display in improper housing. In LaCrosse, Wisconsin, for example, wildlife is kept under deplorable—if not disgraceful—conditions in one of the city's parks. Why the people of this great state allow such atrocities escapes me.

Of course, the roadside zoo problem is not confined to the Badger State. Literally hundreds of RZs exist nationwide. Some states have banned such establishments. Others should, too.

For those who want to see live animal exhibits, there are plenty of real zoos. For the educationally minded, excellent nature programs abound on television.

"Look." Linda pointed to a huge, blondish-brown bear in the next cage. A mammoth Kodiak bear sat on his haunches and leaned against the bars of his cage. He turned his head toward us as we walked by. His native home, the rugged island of Kodiak, Alaska, was thousands of miles away.

"How'd you ever get here?"

"What?" Linda asked. "What'd you say?"

"Ah, nothin'. Never mind. Come on. Let's get out of here."

After we got home, I called Dr. Barnes. His voice was a bit ratchety but there was still some fire there. He rambled on for at least an hour about doctoring wildlife— like the time a lynx bit off his earlobe. Or about the ostrich that kicked him in the back and he passed blood in his urine for over a week. He had a definite knack for telling stories. Then the lively old vet told me something that I should have guessed all along. He wasn't about to quit.

Dr. Barnes's resolve to continue practicing saved me certain agony over a tough question. I sympathized with the animals at the Roundup and truly wanted to help them. But I was struggling with a larger issue. Would

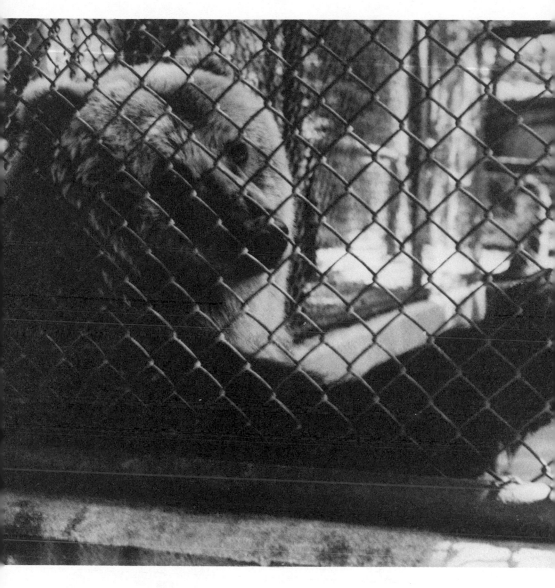

An Alaskan bear looks mournfully from its cage.
This bear should be with others of his kind—
stalking rugged Kodiak Island, his native home.

assisting Orville make me a party to his travesty? Would I be condoning animal exploitation?

I called Mr. Dobson the following morning.

"You won't be needing me. I had a long conversation with Dr. Barnes. He has no intention of quitting."

"He doesn't?" Orville was surprised. "Well, maybe he'll retire next year. Will you consider my offer then?"

"Yeah, maybe next year." I felt safe. I knew something about vets that Orville didn't: ol' Doc Barnes would never retire.

THE
GRAY MOUSE

"C'MON, LIN," I CALLED FROM THE FRONT DOOR. "IT'S ALREADY seven-thirty. It'll be dark in a couple hours. Let's get going." My oversized tackle box felt heavy, so I set it down. "Why does it always take you so long to get ready?" I said under my breath.

"What was that you said?" Linda shouted from the basement.

"Hurry up! We haven't got all day." I was impatient. It was not very often that Linda and I got to go fishing together.

But tonight it was different. For once I wasn't worried about emergency calls. The hospital recording machine had malfunctioned, and the phone company couldn't fix it until tomorrow.

I could hear Linda climbing the basement steps. "Faster," I yelled and laughed. She hated it when I prodded her to hurry. No matter where we went, I was always ready first.

"Stop bugging me, Ror! I'm going as fast as I can. I had to find my sweat shirt." Linda was nearly out of breath.

I picked up my tackle box and minnow bucket and

grabbed the fishing rods. "Here, Lin, you carry the net and boat cushions."

Linda, Tenille, and I left the house for the short walk down to the boat. We didn't live right on Lake Shishebogama, but we had deeded access a block or two away. I kept my boat tied up at the dock there.

Tenille was the first one in the boat. She was more excited than usual. Maybe it was because both Linda and I were going. Normally Tenille and I fished alone. Linda liked to go but wasn't a fishing addict like me. Usually she graciously volunteered to answer the phone when I was out on the lake. If I got a call, she would simply beep my pager and I would return to shore.

"Linda, you sit in the middle. Leave Tenille in the front seat. She's used to sitting there." I set my tackle box within easy reach of the back seat and laid the rods along one side. I held the boat against the dock for stability while Linda settled in. My fishing vessel wasn't exactly roomy, but it was adequate. It was a green fourteen-foot V-hull, made by Starcraft. I had let a neighbor use my boat the month before, and when he returned, he approached the dock too fast. The boat hit the corner of the wooden dock right where the word STARCRAFT was printed on the bow. The letter C was completely scraped off. My boat now read STAR RAFT. Kind of a nice name, I thought.

I pulled on the starter rope. On the third try, the nine-horse Johnson fired. I backed away from the dock and turned around. It felt good to be on the water. Fishing was my absolute favorite hobby. I always liked to say there were two important things in life: one was fishing—the other was planning to go fishing.

"Isn't it great to be out here?" I yelled above the sound of the outboard.

Linda turned toward me. The wind caught her long dark hair and swirled it around her face. Rather than compete with the motor, she simply nodded in agreement.

I pulled on the handle of the motor and we rounded a point, heading toward the big part of the lake. Tenille bounced softly as we crossed the wake of another boat. "Hang on, Neelie," I heard Linda tell her.

The warm, caressing summer wind came directly out of the south—my favorite direction for good fishing. I swung wide and slowed a bit to avoid interfering with a loon and her chick. Once around them, I sped up and headed for East Bay. It wasn't exactly my favorite fishing hole on the lake, but the weedy center bar and the prolific weed growth along the shorelines made the area particularly "fishy."

Shish was a good lake for walleye, musky, northern pike, and bass. Every one of those species liked weeds. We had my favorite wind direction, the right time of day, and a good spot. I was confident that we'd catch something.

"Linda, go to the bow and get ready to drop the anchor," I said as I slowed the motor. "We'll start by the lily pads out here." I stopped the motor near the weeds in the center.

"Tell me when you want me to drop it." Linda held the mushroom-shaped, yellow anchor over the bow.

"Drop," I said. Linda let the anchor down and let the gray rope slide over the gunwale. Hand over hand, she allowed the anchor to slowly descend toward bottom. Hundreds of tiny bubbles rose to the surface. I knew the anchor had hit. I lowered the stern anchor to hold the boat parallel to the weeds.

"Okay, Lin. How do you want to fish? Do you want to cast, or how about a minnow on a bobber? As long as we're anchored, I'd suggest a minnow. We can always cast later."

"Okay. I'll try a minnow if you rig it up." Linda didn't like touching the bait.

I hooked on a wiggly chub for her and threw it out

toward the edge of the pads. Tenille cocked her head slightly and watched the minnow and red and white plastic bobber kerplunk on the water.

"It's about ten feet deep from where your bobber is, Lin. There's a coontail bed down there." Coontail weeds were one of my favorites. They seemed to attract the fish.

A loon's haunting call echoed from the main part of the lake. "I wonder if that's the one we saw," Linda whispered to Tenille.

Linda turned toward me. "You know, I think loons are my favorite bird. Their sound is so mysterious, yet enchanting. I read somewhere that loons have at least four separate calls—a tremolo, a yodel, a wail, and a . . ." She paused. "I forgot the fourth one. You know what else?" Linda didn't let me answer. "Loons have been around for fifty million years. That's a long time."

Intent on discussing loons, Linda was not watching her bobber. "Linda! Pay attention. We're not out here for an ornithology class. Your bobber's down." Linda's lackadaisical fishing attitude bothered me a bit. She had fairly good skills, but I found her attention span somewhat lacking. "We're not out here to enjoy ourselves," I often joked with her. "We're fishing!"

"Now tighten up the line and set the hook," I instructed. The bobber stayed down as Linda followed my directions.

Linda reared back. The six-and-a-half-foot fiberglass rod strained. I could tell by the bend that she had a good fish.

"Reel steadily," I barked. "Not too fast, now. Keep the rod tip up." I always provided play-by-play instructions, which often annoyed Linda.

"Stop telling me all that. I already know all that stuff." Linda grimaced and kept reeling. As the fish neared the boat, the drag began to work.

"The way it's acting, Lin, I'd say you have a nice

walleye. Keep the rod tip up and don't let him have any slack line." I reached for the net.

Several seconds later I netted a three-pound walleye. "Nice job, Lin. Nice job." I gave Linda a pat on the back. I wasn't sure who was more excited—Linda, Tenille, or me.

I glanced over at my bobber. Still not down. "Lin, the walleyes might just be moving in right now. I'll put another minnow on and let's get right back out there."

"Hurry," Linda said. "Get me baited up. I want to throw it out myself this time."

"Okay," I agreed. "But throw it right where you were before. Walleyes often seem to bite in one small spot on a weed bed."

Linda swung the rod back over her head and pushed the button on her reel. Her distance was correct, but she didn't come close to the spot where she'd caught the walleye. Linda's casting ability was suspect, to say the least. Besides accuracy problems, she occasionally didn't pay attention to her back cast. The hook she lodged in my head last year was testimony to this.

"Jeez, Lin, can't you throw any better than that? I told you to throw right back out where you were," I scolded in a low voice. "Reel it in and throw again." I knew that in the boat I didn't have as much patience as I should with Linda. She tried hard, and she did catch fish. But then again, I'd heard my father yell at my mother for fishing improprieties. And my grandfather used to yell at my stepgrandmother in the boat. It was a family tradition—or, perhaps it was genetic. It was out of my control.

"Walleyes don't bite very long, Lin. Let me throw it out again." I took the rod from her hand, reeled up the minnow the rest of the way, and lobbed it back to the spot where she had caught the fish. "There." I handed the rod back to her.

We sat there for a good hour and a half. Linda caught a small northern pike, and I picked up a two-pound walleye. It was almost dark.

"Lin, do you want to stay out longer or go back? It's so nice out here, and the bugs aren't bad. Maybe we ought to stay out awhile after dark. We can't fish like this, but we could go in and cast up there in the corner." I pointed to the corner of the lake where I knew there was a good weed bed. "I've gotten several bass in the past out of that area, Lin. Maybe they'll be in there tonight." I knew if there was any way to get Linda to stay any longer, it was by mentioning the word "bass." We had bass-fished together when we first met, and bass were still her favorite.

Linda looked at me for a second. "Sure. Let's stay out awhile," she agreed.

"We'll move in a few minutes," I said. "But first I have to change our rigs." There was just enough daylight left to do that without using the flashlight. "Reel your minnow in, and I'll put on a new lure for you." I opened my tackle box so she could see inside. "What do you want to try?"

I pulled the top shelf open, exposing the two shelves beneath. The first shelf was divided lengthwise into three long compartments, suitable for holding the larger muskie or northern pike lures. The bottom two shelves were divided the other way; each housed eight or ten lures of smaller size like those used for bass or walleye. Beneath the lure trays was a large bottom bin. The items found here were those not dignified enough to warrant a separate position up above. Hooks of various sizes, sinkers, bobbers, spare reel parts, and the like, were thrown together. There were even a few unproductive old lures of mine that were one step away from not being carried at all.

My favorite Jointed Pikie, its paint long since lost in battle, occupied the most prominent spot in my tackle box—right there on the top shelf. The reason—it had provided my fondest fishing memory. I had landed a twenty-four-pound muskie on it, the largest for me so far. Seated with the Pikie were my yellow Super Hawk, a silver Cisco Kid, and a black Mudpuppy, three more favorites.

On the next two shelves were a variety of proven fish-getters. Plugs or spoons like Little Cleo, Lazy Ike, small yellow Globe, Mepps Minnow, and at least two dozen more filled the spaces. I could become mesmerized looking through my tackle box. And each lure had its own story to tell from fishing trips gone by.

A few lures had never even been used; I had bought them because I liked the sound of their names. Linda didn't appreciate my fascination with my tackle box, and I certainly couldn't tell her I had purchased some lures just because they had intriguing names. She wouldn't understand—a genetic shortcoming, I'm sure.

"Ror, Ror, why are you staring at your tackle box?" Linda's voice jolted me back to reality.

"Staring, who's staring? I'm just looking through here to find the best lures. Do you see what you want to use?" I moved my hand so she could have an unobstructed view of the entire box.

Linda reached down and dug through the bottom bin. "Here," she said. "I think I'll use this." She held up an old Gray Mouse. Two rusty treble hooks dangled beneath the dark-gray wooden body that resembled a mouse. Surprisingly the brittle rubber tail was still attached after all those years. I had never caught much on the Gray Mouse, evidenced by its unfavorable position in the bottom of the box. I guess I hadn't chucked it because the company that made it—Shakespeare Tackle Company of Kalama-zoo—was not far from my hometown.

"Linda, I have better lures than this. I'm not even sure why this old thing is in here. Never caught much on it. It's an old bass lure."

"You said, pick whatever I want, and I want to use

the Mouse," Linda said. I didn't argue. I should have thrown that lure out long ago, I thought to myself. It didn't have good action.

Reluctantly, I tied the Gray Mouse onto Linda's line. I picked a fluorescent orange Rapala for myself, a proven walleye-getter. In near darkness, we hoisted both anchors and headed for the corner of East Bay. As we slowly motored to our destination, Tenille stuck her nose in the air and sniffed at the cool night.

I shut the motor off, and we drifted to about the right spot.

"Cast toward shore, Lin. There are good coontails and cabbage over there. Be prepared for anything. Bass, walleye—anything could be in here." Linda let fly with a cast toward shore while I dunked first one oar, then the other.

"Lin, reel the Mouse in at a fairly steady speed. I'll row us along this way and cast, too. If you feel anything at all, set the hook."

We floated along for fifteen or twenty minutes, enjoying the summer night. It was so dark now that the lures could not be seen in the air or hitting the water. Kersplash was the only clue that the plug had landed safely in the water after a lofty cast toward shore.

"Lin, wait to start reeling till after you hear the lure hit the water. Like this. . . ." I cast toward shore—kersplash. I started reeling. "See?"

"No problem. I can do that." Linda leaned back and threw the Gray Mouse. After what seemed like too long a time, her lure splashed ten feet from the boat.

"Jeez, Lin. I thought you knew how to cast. Keep your finger on the button longer," I preached. "Concentrate."

Linda reeled the line back in and fired again. This time it was perfect. "Why aren't we getting any bites?" she demanded. I could tell she was getting restless.

"Maybe they're not in here. Let's go to the fallen tree. It hangs out over the water just a little farther. It's real hard to see, but if you look, you can barely make out the outline." I pointed down the shore.

The light from the half-moon glowed softly along the side of Linda's face. "Yes, I think I see it. Isn't that where we caught all those bluegills last spring?" she asked.

"Yeah. That's the same spot." Some years ago a towering Norway pine had been struck by lightning. Half the tree was torn away and leaned precariously over the water. Some of the limbs touched the surface of the lake. The other half of the pine still stood straight and tall and blended perfectly with the forest behind.

The lonely cry of a loon pierced the stillness of the bay. A sudden rustling of leaves from the shoreline woods startled Linda.

"What was that noise? . . . I'm glad we're in the boat."

"Probably just a raccoon stirring, or maybe a deer—or possibly a huge bear." I laughed out loud.

The oars creaked as I gave the boat a final push to align us in front of the sagging tree.

"Linda, you throw to the right side, and I'll throw on the left. Whatever you do, don't throw it in the tree." Linda didn't respond. "I don't know how we'd get it out tonight. We'd probably have to break the line. Don't hit the tree," I repeated. Of course, that would be an honorable way to lose that lure, I thought.

I eased back and cast my Rapala alongside the massive pine. Kersplash. I heard it hit and began reeling.

Linda leaned a bit backward and threw. There was silence. The expected splash of the wooden Gray Mouse never occurred.

"For godsakes, Lin—" That was as far as I got.

Linda's scream probably scared every loon on the lake. It certainly scared me. "Something's wrong. Something's got my line." Her voice quivered.

"What are you talking about? You threw into the tree."

Whosh. Whosh. Suddenly I was aware of the thunderous sound of flapping wings. "What the devil—"

"Something's pulling my rod upward." Linda was frantic.

In that instant it dawned on me. Linda had hooked a bird of some sort.

"You hooked a bird!" I yelled. I threw my rod into the bottom of the boat. "Give me your pole."

I grabbed Linda's rod out of her hand. The line momentarily went limp. There was a sudden voluminous splash only about twenty feet from the boat. The lure and line must have interfered with flight. The bird had crashed into the water.

Quickly I reeled in the slack line. We could hear the loud slapping sound of wings on water. The churning sent ripples that could be seen in the dim moonlight.

"What do you think it is, Ror?"

"I don't know, but we're going to have to get the hook out. Grab the oars and row over there." I shouted orders like the captain of a ship.

Linda rowed while I stood in the stern of the boat holding her fishing rod in one hand. I reached down for the flashlight.

In the beam of the light, the eyes of an owl glared like yellow jewels floating on the surface of the water. One ear tuft stood straight up. The water had caused the other to slick down against his head. He was rattled—so were we.

"Lin, you caught an owl. Looks like a great horned." I paused. "Or should I say the owl caught you."

Linda was incredulous. "That's impossible," she said out loud.

"No, it isn't. Look out there." During my fishing days

I had heard of owls snatching lures out of the night air, but I never thought I would see it happen.

"Tenille, stay." Tenille was standing on the front seat and whimpering, as if she might jump overboard. "Tenille, stay," I ordered.

Linda maneuvered the boat to the bird. By this time his waterlogged feathers had taken their toll. He was tiring. He still made an attempt to escape, but not with the gusto I had heard before.

"We're going to have to net him," I decided and said out loud. "The Gray Mouse is no doubt stuck in his feet. He must have grabbed it out of the air when it sailed by him. . . . Unbelievable! Lin, take the net and very carefully scoop him up. It'll keep him from flying out. I'll see if I can get the Mouse out of his feet."

Linda slid the net into the water and under the owl. "Okay, now lift," I said. The aluminum handle of the net bent under the weight of the soaked owl. The great horned snapped his beak angrily.

"Lin, can you hold the net with one hand and the light in the other? I'm going to need two hands to unhook him." Fortunately I knew how to handle owls. This fact made things a lot easier. What, I wondered, would other fishermen do?

I cut several strands from the bottom of the net so that I could reach his feet. "So much for my net," I muttered to Linda.

To prevent injury, I held the owl's legs in my left hand and worked on the lure with the other. Only one hook of the two trebles had penetrated the flesh. The hook had gone all the way through one toe. With my pliers, I snipped off the point and barb and backed out the hook. A speck of bright red blood trickled from the puncture wound. The flow increased, covered the toe, and dripped onto Linda's boat cushion below. I squeezed

the toe until the bleeding stopped. Then I untangled the other hooks and unwound the line from around his talons.

"Lin, lower the net a bit and I'll reach in over the top and get him out of the net. I'll be able to hold him that way. You'll have to row toward shore. He's too wet to fly."

The oars squeaked noisily under Linda's strong pull. Her adrenaline was flowing. The boat came to a sudden halt as we struck bottom in the shallows of the bulrushes.

"Linda, hold Tenille by the collar." Clutching the owl tightly, I stepped into ankle-deep water. I waded the remaining few feet to the shore and placed the owl on a nearby tree limb. Bewildered and still wet, he made no attempt to fly. He'd be fine, though.

Back in the boat, I rowed us out to deeper water and sat down wearily. The whole escapade had lasted less than ten minutes, but it seemed longer. "Can you believe it, Lin? I told you not to use that dumb Gray Mouse."

"I wouldn't believe it if I hadn't been here." Linda paused in a state of near disbelief. "Incredible. That was incredible."

Linda and I sat holding hands in the darkness and rehashed the events of the past few minutes. From time to time, the loon continued his evening concert somewhere in the distance. Hoohoo-hoohoo, hoohoo-hoohooaw. A barred owl called to his mate deep within the woods. Bullfrogs and crickets chimed unharmoniously along with the voices of a hundred other nocturnal creatures.

Wisps of ghostly fog were settling in across the lake.

This great horned owl is the same species as the one the author's wife "caught" while fishing. This one was hit by a car and brought to the hospital.

To keep Linda from chilling in the damp, cool air, I motored back slowly.

Fifty feet from our dock I cut the engine. "Linda, grab the dock when we get alongside it."

Tenille bounded out of the boat onto the dock and stretched. Linda teetered, caught her balance, and then climbed out. She held the boat while I unloaded the gear. I set everything out except my tackle box. I clunked open the top and examined the upper shelf.

"Linda, shine the light down here, would you?" Linda directed the flashlight to my end of the boat. I found the Gray Mouse on the bottom of the boat under her seat. I stared at the old lure and then at my tackle box.

"Come on, Ror, hurry up. The bugs are terrible. What in the world are you looking in your box for *now*?" The light flickered back and forth. Linda was waving off and swatting mosquitoes.

I reached down to the first compartment and slid my favorite Jointed Pikie several inches to the right. I laid the Gray Mouse in its place.

"Ror, come on. What's taking so long?"

I didn't answer. I knew she wouldn't understand.

THE
FIRING LINE

I COULD HEAR THE PHONE RING ABOVE THE HIGH-PITCHED screech of the ultrasonic dental instrument. That was the fourth ring. I continued cleaning what was left of Blazer's teeth. It rang again. Five. Water and bits of tartar sprayed upward. I should have worn a mask, I thought. Blood oozed from the old beagle's molar and ran down the gum. Six. Where was Linda? The vibrating tip stuck momentarily behind the exposed roots of the fourth premolar, the largest tooth in a dog's mouth. Seven. I could feel my neck muscles tighten. Why didn't Linda answer the phone? Eight. I lifted my foot from the control, and the machine's annoying scream stopped.

"Linda . . . the phone!" My shout was probably as annoying. She didn't respond.

Nine. "Lin! Get the phone!" My voice boomed. Even Blazer, who was not far under the anesthetic, involuntarily twitched.

Ten. I heard the "seeing-eye" buzzer. Someone had walked in the front door. "Lin. Is that you?"

Eleven. "I can't talk now. The phone's ringing," Linda yelled.

"You're kidding," I said under my breath. I slammed

my foot back down on the pedal. "You're fired," I whispered. I fantasized about what it would be like to fire my own wife. Would she still do my laundry? And cook? Probably not.

Linda sprinted to the prep room. "It's Fran. And she wants to talk to you."

I stopped cleaning and glared at my wife. "Where were you?" I growled. "Why did it take you so long to get the phone?"

"Oh. How many times did it ring? I was out getting the mail, and Ed Schaub pulled into the parking lot. He wanted to know how everything was going."

I liked Ed. He was the contractor who had built our hospital. "That was nice of him . . . but next time you go outside, take the phone off the hook. It rang eleven times."

I turned back to Blazer and stepped on the switch.

"Ror! Fran wants to talk to you."

I had forgotten. I lifted my foot and turned. The hold light on the phone was blinking. "Lin, you'll have to hold the phone for me. Look at my hands." The surgical gloves I was wearing were covered with blood, saliva, and foul debris from Blazer's mouth.

Linda held the phone to my ear and pushed the button.

"Hi, Frannie. What's up?" I wiped Blazer's tongue with a gauze sponge.

"Hi, Doc. I got one for you." Her hoarse voice crackled. Fran's asthma again. "There's a loon down out here. We're at the airport. He's on the runway and won't fly away."

"Wait a minute. Slow down. You said you're at the airport and there is a loon on the runway?"

"Yes, that's it," Fran puffed. She sounded out of breath. "We gotta do something before a plane lands."

"Hold on a second, Fran." Linda pulled the phone away. I grabbed Blazer's legs and turned him over to do the other side of his mouth. I nodded at Linda and she replaced the receiver.

"Okay, I'm back. Talk loud so I can hear you. I have to clean a dog's teeth." I depressed the foot control and resumed scaling. Linda pressed the phone tighter against my ear, and I continued, "It probably landed this morning after the rain. The runway may have been covered with a film of water. The loon thought it was a lake." I had seen this sort of thing happen before. Loons were easily fooled. Standing water on an airline runway, a parking lot, or a highway must appear like a sizable body of water. Unsuspecting loons crash-land on the hard surface.

Even worse, loons cannot fly unless they take off from open water. Their legs are placed at the rear of their streamlined bodies, where they act as paddles. Except for swimming, their legs are useless. On land loons cannot walk. They lurch and stagger and push themselves along on their bellies. If not rescued, a grounded loon will die.

"I can tell you're busy. Tell us what to do, honey," Fran coaxed. She was always up for an adventure.

"You have to bring it in. Loons slam down so hard when they land that they can injure themselves. It may have broken a leg or wing." I knew that Fran and Maggie could handle the task.

"Can we just go out there and pick it up?" Fran asked.

"Yeah, you can. Just keep your face away from its head. If you want to, you can toss a blanket over him. I'd put him in a cardboard box for the truck ride. He'll be fine."

"Okay, Doc, whatever you say. We'll do it. Maggie and I will be in as soon as we catch 'im." The phone clicked. Fran had hung up.

"I'm done. You can hang up now," I said to Linda.

I finished cleaning Blazer's teeth and trimmed his twisted nails. One bled slightly, so I used a silver nitrate stick to stop the bleeding.

Half an hour later I heard the front-door buzzer. After several seconds, it went off. Then back on. Then off. Then on. Then off. Then it stayed on for at least thirty seconds. There was only one explanation. I dialed the front desk intercom.

"Hi, Lin. Tell Fran and Maggie to take the loon into the first exam room. I'll be there in a second."

Linda laughed. "Okay. I'll tell the rescue unit."

I flung the exam room door open. A large brown box labeled Charmin Tissue perched on the stainless-steel table. Two heads were visible over the top of the box.

"Do you think the box is large enough?" I chuckled.

"I sent Maggie back home to get a box and she came back with this. You'd think we were rescuing a moose." Fran smirked sarcastically. Perspiration tracked down her temples and neck. Her wispy gray hair was damp.

"Well, like I said, that was the first box I could find. You said hurry." Maggie's blue sweat shirt was askew. Her face was flushed.

I reached for the box. "Did he try to peck you?" I glanced back and forth.

"No. In fact, his beak doesn't look quite right. I think he smashed the end of it. We put a blanket over him anyway, so the little devil couldn't get us," Maggie offered. "We named him Crash," she snickered.

I set the box on the floor and unfolded the flaps.

"Be careful, Doc. He's a big feller," Fran warned. Fran and Maggie stood clear and craned their necks to look into the box.

Cautiously, I peered at Crash. Except for a portion of his tail, the loon had wriggled free of the green wool blanket. This water bird was larger than a duck but smaller than a goose. His black back was evenly checkered with white squares, and he was white underneath. The greenish-black head cocked from side to side. The long, thick pointed bill was crushed on the end. Evidently the tip had somehow rammed the pavement when the loon landed.

"Magnificent creature," I said. Loons never failed to impress me.

"Aren't they beautiful? Look at his red eyes," Linda added. She had come into the room for a look.

"What about the beak? Can you fix it?" Maggie inquired.

"Of course he can," Fran interjected. I'm not sure where she got her confidence in me. Maggie maintained her perpetual grin.

"Well, um, I'll think of something." I stared at his beak. The last half-inch of both upper and lower parts was splintered. Instead of sharp points, the ends were flattened. "For now, I think I'll leave Crash in the box until I get the X-ray room ready. I'll take a quick film to make sure that no bones are broken." I straightened. "Why don't I call you guys after a while?" I smiled at Fran and Maggie.

"Okay, honey. We have to get lunch and get back to the kennel right now, anyway. We've got two coming at two o'clock." Fran looked down at her watch.

"By the way, how did you two happen to see the loon way out on the runway?" Linda questioned. "Who saw him first?"

Maggie meekly raised her hand. "I saw him. We were on our way into town, and I spotted something on the east-west runway where it parallels the road. Fran stopped the truck, and I looked through the binoculars. I sure thought it was a loon."

"Yeah, I didn't believe her! I couldn't imagine what a loon would be doing there. But sure enough, she was right," Fran conceded.

"You know, Frannie, Mrs. Morton is coming with

those maniac Dalmatians. Those two are always trying to get out of their runs. Mrs. Morton doesn't like to wait. Come on, we have to go." Maggie was insistent.

"Call us, honey." Fran and Maggie turned to go. "Oh, yeah, we've been watching Lockheed, and he's flying now," Fran said as she walked out the door.

"Linda, would you please set up the X-ray room? One large cassette, tabletop," I requested. "While I'm taking the X ray, give Pete Moss a call. He wants me to call him whenever I get a loon in." Pete's first name was actually Boston, but he had been given the nickname Pete, maybe because of the way the thirty-year-old nature buff lived. As far as work went, he didn't. He didn't need to: he had scads of money—all of it from his parents.

Pete was a self-proclaimed naturalist and an amateur photographer. Truth is, I'm not sure he did much else, even though he always said he was busy.

I always got a kick out of Pete's attitude. He was both self-righteous and disdainful. Disdainful of the very system that provided him with his life-style. He lived off his ancestors' trust fund. From his own Walden, he would venture forth into the real world for anything that suited his purpose—to photograph a loon, for instance. When the locals were real lucky, they might hear this expert on life utter a word or two of wisdom. Henry David would have rolled over.

"Ror, the room is ready." Linda's announcement interrupted my thoughts.

I carried Crash to the X-ray room. I set the loon on the table and examined him. Except for the beak, I could not detect any injury. Since I knew that he would need to be sedated while I worked on his bill, I administered an injectable sedative.

The X rays revealed nothing. All of his bones appeared normal.

I concentrated on his beak. I had thought about

An injured loon rests on the exam room floor. As can be seen in the photo, a loon's legs are positioned for swimming, not walking.

reconstructing the fragments to form the original point. These could be held together with acrylic. On closer examination, however, I realized that many pieces were missing. I had to do something else.

"Linda, bring me the big file from the instrument drawer," I hollered to her. I sat on the table with the loon.

"What do you want?" Linda replied.

"The big file. I have to work on his beak." I hesitated. "Hurry, he won't stay asleep for long."

Linda appeared with the file and gave it to me. "Here, Lin, you hold the body. He's not totally out." I motioned with my hand. "I guess I'm going to have to file new points on his beak. I don't know what else to do." I looked at Lin for some form of reassurance.

"Don't look at me. I'm not the vet," Linda responded.

That's reassuring, I thought. "Thanks for the vote of confidence."

I grasped the upper half of the beak and began to file. With each abrasive stroke, strands and bits of black beak fell to the table. The flattened tip became more round. With a little more rasping, I had fashioned a point that was nearly like the original. Of course, it was at least one inch shorter, but it was still about two and a half inches long. And it would grow back.

"There, Lin, how do you like that? Eight years of college and I can file a beak. Here, feel it." I turned Crash's head toward Linda.

Linda ran her fingers over the new tip. "That's pretty good, Dr. Dolittle. You're a real wildlife doctor," Linda laughed.

I repeated the process on the lower portion of the bill. I fitted the two halves together as well as I could. I was fairly certain the remodeling would not hinder the bird's ability to eat. By the time I finished, the loon was waking up.

I lined a cage with Fran and Maggie's blanket and placed the patient inside to fully recover. Just in time to skip lunch and start the afternoon appointments.

Pete Moss arrived about an hour later. Linda escorted him back to Crash's cage. Pete's shriek could be heard throughout the hospital. I had difficulty explaining the source of the scream to the owner of a Brittany spaniel.

"Oh, you mean Pete Moss. Does he work for you?"

"No, he's here visiting a patient."

"That figures. I didn't think he had a job."

As soon as I was finished with the Britt, I hurried back to the loon.

"What happened to his beak?" Pete's voice hurt my ears.

"Keep your voice down, will you? There are clients up front." I looked at Pete's long beard and ruddy face. He wore a blue and yellow woodsman's shirt, L. L. Bean khakis, and Maine hunting boots.

"His beak. It's too short." Pete's dark-brown eyes riveted on the loon.

"Fran and Maggie found him on one of the runways at the airport. He must have landed this morning after the rain. The beak hit the pavement and the tip was completely destroyed. I sharpened it again. What do you think? How does it look to you?"

Pete laughed and gaped at the bird. "You fool bird, why did you land there? No wonder they call you guys loons."

"He may look peculiar, but he'll survive."

"When are you going to let him go?" Pete asked.

"Well, the Department of Natural Resources wants to know whenever I get a loon in, so I called them a while ago. I told them that I would gladly take the loon to a secluded lake. You know, give him a chance to be left alone." I pointed to the patient. "But you know the DNR.

They told me that someone would be over in the morning to pick him up. They insisted on releasing him themselves. I'm not sure why they won't let me release the loon." I paused. "But then, maybe they do have the perfect spot for it."

"Do you mind if I take a few pictures? My cameras are in the car." Pete was excited.

"Cameras? Did you say 'cameras'? How many do you have?"

Pete thought for a moment. "Counting my underwater Nikon, I have five, but I don't have them all with me."

"Of course, I don't mind. Take as many pictures as you want. You can even take him out of the cage—or outside." I said. "I'll be up front if you need me." I turned around and left.

Between appointments I notified Fran of the good prognosis and pending release.

Pete stayed for a good hour and a half. I was in the exam room when he departed. He told Linda he was too busy to take any more photographs today, but would return in the morning.

"He's coming back with a new lens. He has to get some close-ups," Linda told me.

"Well, he could have come right back tonight. We'll be here until at least seven." I looked at my watch. It was 5:00 P.M. Appointments lasted until 6:00, and then it would take an extra hour to do treatments and clean up.

"He couldn't come right back because a friend was coming over to look at his new Old Town canoe."

"Old Town canoe? I've always wanted an Old Town," I lamented. "Yeah, that Pete sure is busy." I looked at Linda. We had gotten up at 5:00 A.M., and we were in the clinic by 6:30. My first appointment was at 8:00, and I hadn't stopped all day. Neither of us had eaten lunch, and we'd be there until 7:00 P.M. I thought about the contrast.

"You know, Lin, I wouldn't trade lifestyles with Pete for one second," I resolved. I liked the vet's life.

The buzzer sounded. Another client. It was time to finish the day.

At 6:30 the next morning Linda and I were greeted at the clinic by Crash's quavering melody. The haunting sounds of his repertoire were indistinguishable to me. But not to Linda.

"Stop." She grabbed my arm on our way across the parking lot. "That's the wail he's doing now. It's usually heard when a mother is separated from her chick or when a mate fails to return after a long absence. He wants to interact with other loons." Linda held my arm.

"How do you know that?" I looked at her.

"Listen," Linda demanded. I turned an ear toward the building. It sounded like a demented woman locked in the hospital. No wonder Indian legend has it that the loon's laughing cry was thought to be the spirits of departed warriors forbidden entry into heaven. The hair on the back of my neck bristled. "There! That's the tremolo. Loons usually do that when they are disturbed or frightened. He wants out." My wife was intense.

I started walking toward the clinic. "Come on, Lin. He'll get his wish shortly. Someone from the DNR is coming at nine."

"Don't you just love loons, Ror?" Linda was excited. "They're so special."

I stuck the key in the lock of the front door. The loon was still calling. "Yeah, they are really something."

I put Crash into a large tub filled with cold water and sent Linda to the bait shop for his breakfast.

Crash's mended bill worked to perfection. I did feel a pang of remorse when I dumped the minnows into the tub. But the loon had to eat, and it's nearly impossible to entice a loon to eat anything but live food. And releasing this avian submarine would sentence countless thousands of minnows to the same fate. I didn't have the answers.

Fran and Maggie arrived at 8:30, and Pete followed shortly.

"His beak is a little short but it works okay in the tub. It'll work in the lake, too." I pointed out my handiwork to the ladies.

"Can I get some close-ups while he's in the water? My mother uses my pictures as models for her paintings," Pete piped up.

I went back into the kennel to take care of the dog and cat patients. Every few moments I could hear the shutter of Pete's camera click. Fran and Maggie ogled the loon. A few minutes later the phone rang in the prep room. I could tell by the ring that it was the intercom.

"Fran," I hollered from the kennel, "can you get that?"

"Hello," I heard Fran blare into the phone. "All right honey, I'll tell him." She hung up and walked into the kennel.

"The guy from the DNR is up front. Do you want me to tell him to come back and get the loon?"

"Yeah, Fran, go ahead." I finished hosing down a dog run.

Moments later I went to the prep room. Pete was talking to a man in an olive outfit. The name "Len" was stitched in red lettering above the left pocket of the uniform. His pudgy body seemed to fill the corner of the room. His short, stout fingers fidgeted nervously at his sides.

"What are *you* doing here?" I heard Pete say. I could tell the two men knew each other. "You're not here for the loon, are you?" Pete was aghast.

"Er, um, they told me to pick up a loon." Len shifted his weight from one foot to the other. His large nose turned red.

"For the loon. You're here for the loon?" Pete could hardly believe his ears. "I thought they'd send a warden or a biologist." Pete wheeled around and faced me. "Rory, this guy is just a maintenance man—a groundskeeper."

I looked at Len. I was as shocked as Pete but at the same time felt embarrassed for this delegate from the DNR. There is nothing wrong with being a groundskeeper. Maybe he was a good groundskeeper. Besides, I thought, at least *he* has a job.

"No big deal. The loon will be just as free—no matter who lets him go." I tried to appease Pete.

"Yeah, but he's a groundskeeper—not a loon expert," Pete protested.

I heard the cigarette lighter click. Fran always lit up a Parliament when she was agitated. "Why don't you let Rory handle it," Fran gruffed and scowled at Pete.

"Where are you going to release him?" Pete tried a different tack.

Perspiration beaded on Len's brow. His neck was blotchy red. "They told me to take it to the public landing on Madeline."

"On Madeline!" Pete bellowed. "Madeline. That's one of the busiest lakes up here. What about all those motorboats and skiers?" Pete continued his barrage.

Why did they have to pick Madeline Lake? Just when I thought I had Len bailed out. I tried to conceal my anger. There were scads of other lakes quieter than Madeline. Why didn't the DNR just let me release it? Why did they hassle me? They always had to have the last word. One thing was for sure: as far as the DNR would know, this would be my last loon.

"Well, the loon can always fly to another lake." I tried once again to defend the groundskeeper.

Fran coughed and hacked. "He'll be all right, Pete. Let him take 'em."

Pete was outnumbered and momentarily relinquished his argument. He left without so much as a good-bye to any of us. I helped Len put the loon into the crate he had brought along. I could tell that he was uncomfortable with the bird.

"Don't worry about a thing," I reassured Len. "When you get to the landing just dump him in the water. He'll swim away." I hesitated, then added, "Don't forget to let him out of the crate before you dump him in." I laughed. So did Len.

"By the way, I apologize for the way Pete talked to you. I know this is not your doing." I tried to put Len at ease.

"Don't worry about him. Pete thinks he's hot stuff." Fran flicked her ashes into the vacated tub.

Finally the debacle was over. Everyone left. The hospital was quiet again.

Linda had been typing at the front desk during the debate over Crash. I related what had happened, especially Pete's arrogance toward Len.

"I have to agree that they should not have sent a maintenance man to release the loon and Madeline Lake is a poor choice . . . but it's not catastrophic and certainly was not worth berating Len," I said and looked at Linda.

"I'm glad I wasn't there. Len looked like a nice man," Linda replied.

"Len is nice. He was just caught in the middle. It wasn't his fault." I thought about Pete for a moment. "Linda, I know that all children of financially successful parents don't grow up to be unambitious. But it seems like an awful lot do. I sure hope our kids don't end up like that."

"You may not have to worry," Linda teased.

"What do you mean?" The phone rang.

"Maybe you won't be successful." Linda snickered and slugged me in the arm. She dashed for the phone.

"You're fired . . . again," I muttered.

EXOTIC
PROBLEMS

I WAS STROLLING THROUGH THE KENNEL TALKING TO THE dogs and cats and enjoying a cup of coffee when Linda found me.

"It's Barbara Eastman. You know her; she's the one with all the cats. She's crying and wants to talk to you." Linda was concerned.

I did know Barbara. She had been a good client since we opened. My only complaint, if I had one, was that she was sometimes overly concerned with her six felines. I don't know how many calls she had made to me after hours, but she averaged at least one a month. Most times, there was nothing at all the matter.

"Did she tell you what she wanted?"

"No, but she's very upset." Linda handed me Barbara's records. "She's in the first exam room."

I marched up front and opened the door.

"Hi, Barb. What's wrong?" I noticed immediately that her usual immaculate appearance had been ignored. The collar of her red plaid blouse was up on one side and down on the other. Rather than neatly placed barrettes in her styled black hair, she sported a makeshift ponytail.

Her eyes were red from crying, and she held a tissue over her delicate nose.

"I should have taken your advice. I should have taken your advice," she sobbed. "You told me not to buy a wild cat. I should have listened."

I knew what Barb meant. She had called me the previous summer to ask about buying a bobcat from a roadside zoo. It was not uncommon in Wisconsin for roadside zoo owners to sell wild animals to the public. The permit necessary to keep a wild animal for a pet was becoming increasingly difficult to obtain, but it was still too easy. Oftentimes, the roadside zoo owner didn't care anyway. If people had the cash, they could buy the animal, no questions asked.

I had told Barb what I told everyone who inquired: stick with dogs, cats, horses, or any other already-domesticated friend. She apparently hadn't listened.

"What happened? Did you buy the bobcat?"

She managed a meek response. "Yes, they were so cute and lovable. And Critter Haven only charged me four hundred dollars." She sniffled. "I knew you wouldn't like it. That's why I didn't tell you."

"Well, what happened? What's wrong?" I felt sympathetic, but at the same time, I was upset with her.

"Tawny killed Mrs. Pfizemont." She started crying again. Mrs. Pfizemont was her prize twelve-year-old Angora. A year earlier I had pulled the cat through a particularly bad bout of pneumonia.

"I'm sorry to hear that." I handed Barbara a wad of paper towels to replace her soaked tissue.

"I can't keep him. Tawny is getting wild, and he's already bigger than my cats. He's too rough. He scratched my nephew two weeks ago, and Bobby needed five stitches."

I wanted to shout, "I told you so," but I didn't. The story was familiar—the outcome inevitably the same. I knew what Barb's next request would be. I'd been there before. I waited.

"I called Critter Haven, and they can't take Tawny back. I called every zoo I could think of. . . . No one wants him. I called the DNR, and they said he cannot be released. I have to have him put to sleep." She rubbed her eyes with a paper towel. "Will you take care of it?"

I hesitated. My hospital policy was that no animal would be destroyed unless, and only unless, it was suffering irreversibly. But Barb was correct. I knew from past experience that there weren't any alternatives. No one wanted a ten-month-old bobcat. Roadside zoos certainly didn't. Real zoos don't need them.

"I'll see what I can do," I assured her. "Do you have him with you?"

"Yeah, he's in a cage out in the car." She got up to go.

"Wait, I'll get him." I grabbed her arm. "Sit back down, I'll take care of it." I started to exit. "You still have the Lincoln, right?" She nodded.

I carried the cage containing Tawny and set him in the isolation ward, away from the dogs and cats. Still tearful, Barbara finally made her way out of the hospital. I had to feel sorry for her.

I tended to regular hospital appointments for the rest of the morning. It wasn't until about 1:00 P.M. that I found time to carry out Barbara Eastman's wishes. I filled a syringe with euthanasia solution and made my way back to the isolation ward. Linda didn't follow.

I sat down on a footstool in the cramped room. Tawny stretched and eyed me curiously. His luxurious grayish-tan coat was flecked here and there with black spots. His short, stubby tail had several black bars on top and was tipped with black. His upper legs were spotted with small, dark blotches. Tawny's face was a bit more brown than the rest of his body and was streaked with broken black lines that radiated into a broad cheek ruff. His erect ears were slightly tufted. I guessed Tawny's weight to be about fifteen pounds, though his thick fur made a weight estimate difficult. He was a beautiful creature.

While I sat there studying him, he rubbed his head on the side of the cage nearest me, apparently seeking attention. I stood up and stepped toward the cage. Tawny recoiled into the corner of his cage and emitted a low growl. His white fangs were visible through his partially open mouth. I thought he might hiss or spit, but he did neither.

Seconds later, he was back at the front of the cage rubbing again. I held my hand toward him. This time he raised a paw as if he wanted to lash out. His lethal claws extended, and his ears flattened.

It was obvious that Tawny was confused in a way he couldn't understand. His reflexes and instincts were simply too deep-seated to have been washed away by Barbara's attempts at domestication.

Watching him posture in the cage made me realize how he might have killed Mrs. Pfizemont. The Angora may have made a sudden movement at the wrong time. Tawny's protective instincts were just beneath the surface, ready to explode at any instant. That's how he must have scratched the child, too.

I looked at the deadly syringe in my hand. There's no way that I would be able to get close enough to give an IV injection, I thought. Tawny would have to be sedated first. I laid the syringe down.

I scrounged through the clinic until I found some meat scraps that I kept on hand for hawks and owls. I hid several tranquilizer tablets in a piece of raw meat and returned to Tawny's ward. He gobbled the tasty morsel as soon as I dropped it through the bars to his cage floor.

I sat down again on the stool and waited for Tawny to become sleepy. I leaned back against the wall and

thought about the circumstances that had led to this moment. If anything peeved me in veterinary medicine, it was people who kept wild animal pets.

In veterinary lingo, any animal kept as a pet other than the usual domesticated species is called an exotic. As Critter Haven exemplified, the exotic pet industry is poorly regulated. Even where regulations exist, they are infrequently enforced. Dealers routinely sell as pets animals that are impossible to domesticate, dangerous, and difficult to keep alive. They entice prospective buyers with misleading statements regarding the animal's care, feeding, and desirability as a pet. Gullible individuals are hooked by the seller's deceptive sales pitch and the cute, lovable appearance of the baby animal. The docility of the newborn does not last long.

The dangerous consequences of the exotic pet trade flash through the news continually. Just the month before, a three-month-old infant had been killed in Michigan when an adult pet raccoon crawled into the baby's crib and bit the child. In another case in Pennsylvania, a pet raccoon attacked a one-year-old boy and chewed his lips and nose off. The family had owned the raccoon for five years.

In New Jersey, a fifty-five-year-old woman had died after she contracted a deadly intestinal infection from her spider monkey. A Georgia veterinarian had recently spent several months in the hospital after catching a rare form of hepatitis from a client's chimpanzee. Still another

Like all wild cats, bobcats make unsuitable pets. No one can provide the environment necessary for raising a physically and mentally normal wild animal.

veterinary assistant came down with Salmonellosis after exposure to an infected chimp.

In Texas, a man caught anthrax from a mountain lion that he purchased from a roadside zoo. In California, a leopard attacked her owner. By the time the leopard was done, the lady needed over three hundred stitches, most of them in her face and right arm. She still does not have full use of her hand. A two-year-old boy in Ohio was killed by a pet lion. The lion dragged the child nearly a quarter-mile through a swamp thicket.

In my own practice, two months before, a supposedly tame timber wolf had—for no apparent reason—savagely attacked his owner. The elderly man, who had kept wolves for a number of years, was bitten in the neck. Only massive amounts of transfused blood saved his life.

An entire family of six were recently forced to go through the painful and very expensive rabies prophylaxis after their pet skunk developed the feared disease.

A fifteen-year-old girl lost one eye to an ocelot, probably the most commonly purchased wild cat. The girl now has a prosthetic eye.

Besides presenting a danger to their owners and others, exotic pets are often in danger themselves. There is a special—if unintentional—kind of cruelty that wild animals kept as pets endure. Virtually no one can provide the type of environment necessary to raise a contented, healthy, well-adjusted wild animal.

Two years before, veterinarians in Miami were inundated with calls from new owners of South American baby anteaters. Most of the animals were critically ill from dietary deficiencies and diarrhea. An investigation revealed that a boatload of the young anteaters had recently made its way into area pet shops. Knowing full well that this animal is nearly impossible to keep in captivity, greedy dealers advertised them as the latest thing in exotic pets and assured prospective buyers that the anteater required little care. A university study later showed that every single anteater had died within one month after its purchase. Further, for every baby anteater that arrived on the ship, three more had died en route.

In Beaverton, California, a black bear was seized after spending the first three years of his life chained near the front of a gas station. The owner kept it because "the bear attracted customers." The chain was imbedded so far into the right front leg that amputation was necessary.

Near Houston, a person reported to the local humane society that his neighbor's pet cougar looked "emaciated and sick." The severely bowlegged animal was suffering from an advanced case of rickets. The surprised owner had been feeding him tuna macaroni exclusively. The cougar was destroyed.

Some owners realize they cannot properly care for their exotic pet and simply give up. In Columbia, South Carolina, a monkey was found badly burned from a jaunt along a high-voltage power line. Police found out that the monkey had been given away in a pet store promotion, but the winner couldn't care for it and had simply released the monkey.

Indeed, research shows that a wild animal pet has little chance of living a full life. According to the Society for the Prevention of Cruelty to Animals, 60 percent of all exotic pets die within one month. Of the remainder, 20 percent die within the first year, and by the end of the second year, only 10 percent are alive. Many wild animals have extremely demanding survival requirements. Owners are seldom, if ever, able to provide the proper temperature control, ventilation, space, or food. A large number of wild animals simply cannot tolerate the smothering affection that an owner would normally heap on a puppy or kitten.

Even reptiles have a shockingly shortened life span in captivity. Despite potential life spans of 25 to 125 years, captive reptiles live an average of less than three years as pets or zoo exhibits.

For exotic pets, getting to the dealer is more than half the danger. For every animal that makes it to the window of a pet shop, eight others die on the way there. In other countries, natives capture the infant animals in the easiest way they can—by killing the parents.

Most animals are captured before they are weaned. Rough handling, unsanitary conditions, extreme temperature changes, and minimal food and water exact a massive toll on young animals. Exporters know this and consequently ship many more animals than they expect to arrive.

Birds are particularly vulnerable to the stresses of capture and shipment. Martin C. Edwardo, an ASPCA administrator, reported on a shipment of over one hundred mynah birds to Los Angeles. Of the original one hundred, only five remained alive.

I wasn't sure what compelled the Barb Eastmans of the world to own exotic pets. Misplaced ego? Status symbol? Fad crazy? There are nearly 150 breeds of dogs available, plus about 40 breeds of cats, along with horses, goats, and many species of fully domesticated birds. Even worse, upwards of ten million would-be loyal dogs and cats die each year in the United States for one reason— they simply need a home. Considering the risks, the problems, and the inevitable cruelty, there is absolutely no reason for any private citizen to own a wild animal.

Tawny yawned audibly. The tranquilizers were working. I studied this magnificent wild cat. His proud head rested on his massive paws. Like most cats, bobcats have developed a unique manner of walking, perhaps as an adaptation to stalking. The cat, because it is able to see where to place its front feet noiselessly, steps in the exact same spots with the hind feet. The resultant bobcat track is very narrow, almost as if it were made by a two-legged animal.

I reached down and picked up the syringe. Tawny was probably quiet enough for me to administer the fatal injection. But I stopped.

I was familiar with numerous reports of family cats being inadvertently left behind by seasonal residents. Cats have an uncanny propensity for being off in the woods when the moment of departure arrives. Amazingly, many of the domestic felines would be waiting on the cottage steps when the owners returned—sometimes months later. Being a vet, I was called upon to examine several of these wayward cats each year. On at least two occasions, domestic cats had survived six months or more on their own, even in remote areas without nearby houses.

If a housecat could make it, certainly a bobcat could.

And it was March. A new winter was months away.

But the DNR had forbidden it. And I had to agree—in principle. After all, a pet bear released back to the wild might pose a threat to campers. Even a "tame" wolf might have great difficulty finding a pack to accept him.

But cats were solitary—and survivors.

It took over an hour on dirt roads to wind my way through the Chequamegon National Forest to a particularly wild and remote stretch of terrain where I had seen bobcat tracks in the past. The early spring thaw had wreaked havoc on the one-lane road. But for my four-wheel drive, I never would have made it. The ruts were so bad that I knew no one else would be foolish enough to drive it—at least for a while.

I carried the cage over a knoll to the edge of a dense poplar thicket. The gushing sound of Moose Skin Creek—my favorite brook-trout stream, now swollen to capacity by melting snow—echoed from over the next hill.

I placed the cage on the ground. By now the sedative

was wearing off. Tawny's eyes still looked a little droopy and red, but I knew that he'd be normal within hours.

I unlocked the cage and eased open the door. Tawny took a tentative step. His head emerged from the cage. I screamed and gave a jolting kick to the cage. Tawny leaped out, somersaulted, regained his footing, and was gone in a shot.

"There. Now stay away from us humans," I yelled.

For a long time, I second-guessed myself. Had I done the right thing? Or had I sentenced Tawny to an even crueler fate? Would he starve or be killed anyway? Had I made an error?

I would never know.

DUNN IN

I PEERED INTO THE STAINLESS-STEEL CAGE. BEFORE ME STOOD one of the most magnificent creatures I had ever seen—a snowy owl. The white owl must have stood nearly two feet tall. Its large yellow eyes were set in a perfectly round head. Asymmetrical, short black bars of plumage dressed his body, from his neck down to his feet. Small tufts of white feathers guarded each side of his dark beak, and heavy feathering protected his legs and feet.

His color and dense insulation were obvious adaptations to his survival in the far North. Snowies nest in the Arctic and, unlike most other owls, will lay their eggs in small scooped-out depressions in the ground. These large and powerful owls are so well adapted for northern living that they rarely migrate south of the Canadian border, even in winter.

This year, though, was different. A large forest fire the summer before in Ontario—the smoke of which was seen all the way down here in northern Wisconsin—had decimated the owls' food supply. For this reason, the Northwoods had experienced an influx of the hungry snowies. They came in January and stayed until late March.

The one in the cage had been found in Jill Breitzman's yard in St. Germain, a small burg about a dozen miles east of Minocqua. Jill had found the bird sitting in her backyard the morning after an extremely foggy March night. The brave young woman had picked up the injured owl and transported him to my animal hospital. X rays revealed a shattered wing and dislocated shoulder.

The only chance the patient had of ever returning to the Arctic was if the shoulder could be replaced and the humerus wired together. It was going to be a tough surgery, but I wasn't too worried. T. J. Dunn was due to arrive within the hour to help me. When it came to bones, he was the expert. T.J. liked helping me with the wildlife. Besides, my periodic calls provided him a respite from traditional small-animal practice.

My first employer was also a prankster of sorts, which made his visits even more fun. We got along famously. During my first month of practice, he had called me into the kennel where he appeared to be taking a dog's temperature. My mentor was crouched down in a run behind a large Saint Bernard.

"What do you want me for?" I asked T.J.

"Could you just hold this guy's head for me so he doesn't get up. Only a few more seconds and I'll have his temperature." T.J. held the dog's tail with his left hand and had the rectal thermometer in place with his right.

"Sure. What's the matter?" I stooped down and held the dog's collar.

T.J. didn't answer. He removed the thermometer from the dog and held it up to the light. Brown, thick

The author's friend, T. J. Dunn,
holds a canine patient.

fecal matter adhered firmly to nearly the full length of it. Small hunks of lighter material also clung to the outside. T.J. inserted the thermometer in his mouth, closed his lips tightly, and withdrew it—totally cleaned off.

"Looks like he has a fever," T.J. coolly remarked.

I let go of the collar and dashed across the room for the tub. I leaned over and gagged. Nothing came up.

T.J. exploded in boisterous laughter. His white teeth contrasted with his Colorado tan. His slightly flattened round nose crinkled. He bent forward, holding on to his stomach. The brown hair that he normally swirled over his bald spot fell out of its designated place. He guffawed for at least five minutes.

T.J. had set me up. His hand had been hidden behind the massive dog. It only appeared as if he was taking the dog's temperature. The thermometer was covered with Skippy chunky peanut butter.

I had tried to repay him for that trick, but each time I pulled something, he'd get me back. The last time I visited his clinic in Rhinelander, I had taken a call for him while he was in surgery.

"Dr. Dunn speaking," I pretended to the caller. T.J. glanced up from the surgery. Halfway through a spay and donned in full surgical garb, he was helpless to intervene.

"Oh, Mrs. Bradley, you've never been here before. You say your dog has been limping for a week?" I said into the phone. I looked at T.J. Mrs. Bradley had never met Dr. Dunn, therefore would not realize that it wasn't him on the phone. I had my cohort where I wanted him.

"Well, Mrs. Bradley, I'm glad you called." She then explained that she couldn't come in till tomorrow. "That'd be fine. I'll look at Bowser in the morning. In the meantime, I want you to do something for me. Give him one-half aspirin at eight o'clock tonight. Then call me at home at 2:00 A.M. to let me know how he's doing."

T.J. looked frantic. Blotches of red started to appear on his neck—a sure sign that he was upset. Like me, he dreaded late-night phone calls.

"No, of course that won't be too late. I'm always up at two," I convinced Mrs. Bradley. "Now I want you to promise you'll call me tonight."

She promised. I hung up. I enjoyed a moment of glee.

T.J. arrived at my hospital on schedule. Together we prepared the owl for surgery. To administer fluids, we inserted an IV line into a vein in the owl's uninjured wing. Because the surgery promised to be a long one, we used inhalation anesthetic. We inserted an endotracheal tube, intended for use in a human infant, into the snowy's trachea. He could safely breathe the gas for hours.

I was lucky to have T.J.'s help. The bone in the wing had splintered into four pieces. I assisted while T.J. delicately put the parts back together. By the time he was done with the fracture, he had used two steel pins running inside the full length of the bone and had tightly wrapped five wires around it.

After the break had been repaired, we turned our attention to relocating the shoulder.

"Hard to imagine all this damage from an antenna." T.J. looked skeptical.

"Not really. I've seen them worse than this. Birds can fly pretty fast." I had treated a number of birds in the past that had collided with antennas or power lines. Especially during inclement weather, birds simply can't always see the narrow wires. They crash right into them, often breaking bones or dislocating joints.

It took both of us to manipulate and hold the damaged shoulder together. T.J. held the wing in place while I sutured. After a few minutes, all that was left to do was to sew the muscle and skin over the joint. That was a one-

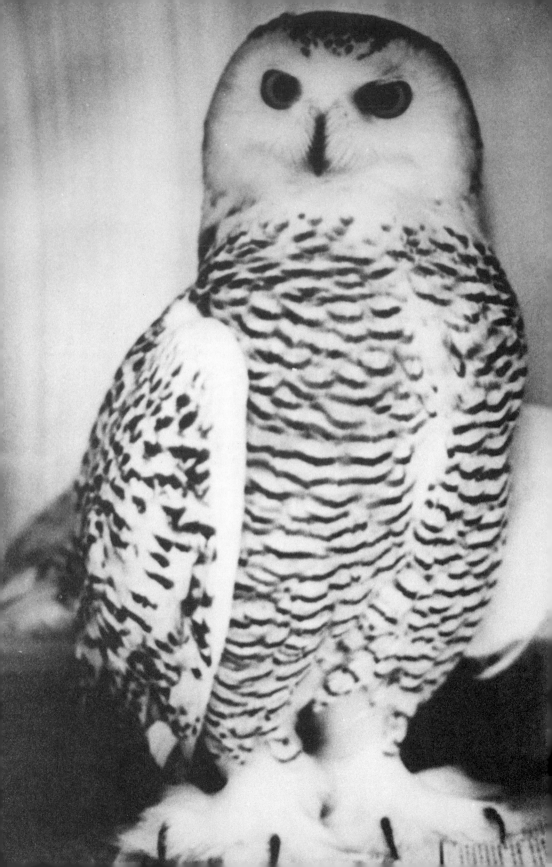

man job. Since T.J. had done most of the work, I volunteered to close. The anesthetic had been turned off five minutes earlier. I knew the bird would wake up soon. I had to hurry.

"Are you done yet, Ror?" Linda hollered from the prep room. "I've got someone on hold. She needs to talk to you." Linda had been answering the phone while we worked on the bird.

"About another five minutes. Who is it?" I answered.

"It's Mrs. Primerose. She's never been here before." Linda giggled and looked embarrassed. "Her dog and the neighbor's dog are stuck together in her front yard." Linda couldn't hold back. Her giggling turned to outright laughter, and her face reddened.

Those kinds of calls were always rather embarrassing. We got four or five each year. Because of the male dog's anatomy, male and female would often lock together during mating. No amount of outside coaxing could separate them. All an upset owner could do was wait.

All of a sudden, T.J. sprang out of the surgery room. "I'll take it. I'll take the call." He grabbed the phone off the wall and pushed the button.

"Oh, thanks, T.J." Linda had no idea what T.J. was about.

"Hi, this is Dr. Foster. Can I help you?" I could see the mischief in his blue eyes. I cringed. Linda looked confused.

T.J. remained silent while Mrs. Primerose explained her predicament.

"Well, what I always like to recommend first is a good dousing with cold water. Have you sprayed them with the

His wing on the mend, a beautiful
snowy owl recuperates in the hospital.
This bird of prey may have a wing-
span of five feet or more.

hose?" T.J. paused. I rolled my eyes. I would never suggest that.

"Oh, you tried that, huh? The next thing I like to recommend is to beat them a little with a broom." T.J. waited again for her answer. I grimaced. Linda stared at T.J. in disbelief.

"Oh, you already have hit them with a broom, huh?" T.J. was matter-of-fact. "Well, the last thing I suggest you do is haul your phone as far outside as you can get it. Put it right next to the dogs. Then hang up. I'll call you back. Let the phone ring three or four times. That should end the romance." T.J. paused again.

"Yes, that's right," T.J. instructed. "I don't know why you don't believe me. I can guarantee it. It works with my wife, Linda, and me every time." T.J. winked at Linda.

Her face was crimson. Her mouth dropped open and she stumbled backward against the wall. I winced.

Then, holding the receiver in his hand, T.J. stepped away from the phone. The line that Mrs. Primerose had called on was still flashing. T.J. had pushed a different button. He had not talked to the woman at all.

Sixty-three days later Mrs. Primerose's champion Scottie had four healthy half-beagle puppies. On the same day, the snowy owl leaped upward from my arm and headed back home. I hadn't yet gotten even with T.J.

BUSYBODIES

LINDA READ THE LETTERING ON THE SIDE OF THE STRAW-colored gunnysack: "Wisconsin Potatoes." She glanced from the sack to the teenage boy holding it. His uncombed blond hair still bore the circular indentation of the now absent cap. A smudge mark streaked from the middle of his forehead to his left eyebrow. Adolescent whiskers poked here and there from his long chin.

"I've got to see the doctor," he finally managed to say. His eyes roved nervously from the front door to Linda and back. "My mom is waiting for me outside in the car." He leaned back to look out the door and into the parking lot, as if to make sure his mother was still there.

Linda wrinkled her nose at the putrid odor that filled the air. "You can't possibly have fish in that bag," she joked. Linda detected a slight movement in the bottom of the bag. Suddenly she realized that there was something alive in there.

"What's in the bag?" Her curiosity was aroused.

The boy's eyes danced about the reception room. He would not look directly at Linda. "I'm here to see the doctor."

"Well, why don't you go into the exam room and I'll get Dr. Foster." The boy clung tightly to the gunnysack and followed Linda.

Linda found me tending to a sick kitten back in the isolation ward. "Ror, there's one up. First exam room. There's a kid in there with something in a gunnysack. He only wants to talk to you. I'm not sure why he's so secretive."

"Did you get the basic info? You know—his name and what he's here for?"

"Not really. I think you'd better talk to him."

I placed the feline patient back on the heating pad and walked up front into the exam room. "Hi, I'm Dr. Foster." I held my hand toward the boy.

We shook. I could see dirt caked under his fingernails. He didn't offer his name.

"What's your name?" I studied him and then the sack.

He seemed reluctant, but finally spoke. "My name is Jesse Gatlin." He hesitated and looked away. "But don't tell anyone."

Linda was right. There was something unusual going on here. "What do you mean, 'don't tell anyone'? Don't tell anyone what?" I wasn't sure what he meant.

"That I was here. My mom said that vets have to keep things secret—like doctors. She called if confa-something."

"You mean, confidentiality?" I cut in. What did he mean, "like doctors"! I felt like telling him that getting into vet school was as hard as or harder than getting into med school. And just as long. But I didn't.

"Yeah, that's it. That's the word."

"Well, your mother is correct. I won't tell anyone about your visit." I stopped for a second, then added, "But my wife. Can I tell my wife? She's the one you met when you walked in."

"Oh, her. Yeah, that's okay. But my mom is worried

about other people finding out. She thinks I might get in trouble." Jesse held the sack toward me.

"Smells like fish in there," I laughed, hoping to take the edge off the conversation.

"There was—but there is somethin' else in there now, a . . . a beaver," he stammered. "I speared a beaver last night. By accident. It was an accident."

"What? A beaver?" I set the sack on the table and began to roll the top down. "Did you say you speared a beaver?" I thought I must have misunderstood.

Jesse nodded but didn't say a word.

The fish odor was almost too much to bear. I leaned back and opened the door. "Let's let a little air in here."

By now I had reached the bottom of the gunnysack. I was used to medical unpleasantries, but this one made even me wince. A young beaver lay in the bottom with his eyes half-closed. His dense brown fur was flecked here and there with what I thought was dried fish slime, evidence of the bag's previous occupants. The smell was staggering. That was only for starters.

Far worse were the two obvious tears in the beaver's side. A loop of purplish black intestine protruded out of the bottom wound. Odoriferous exudate oozed from the holes. The patient flailed his legs weakly. At least he was alive. I swung away from the exam table to catch my breath.

"What happened? Tell me exactly what happened." I looked at Jesse.

Before he could respond, I stuck my head out of the exam room and called to Linda. "I have to get an IV started. Bring me the stuff."

Jesse Gatlin stared at the beaver and began to talk. "Last night me and another kid went spearin' suckers down at Rocky Run Crick. A dark shadow came out from the bank about three feet underwater. I thought it was a fish of some kind so I speared it. But it was him." He pointed to the beaver. "I didn't know what to do so I shook him off into the sucker bag. I took him home, but Mom wouldn't let me call you during the night, so we waited till today."

I believed his story. Each spring spawning suckers swim up streams and rivers, making them accessible to the spear fisherman. The best time to go is at night when the suckers are moving the best. Smoked or pickled suckers are considered by some to be an epicurean delight. It was possible that in the current of a stream, and with only lantern light, Jesse and his friend had made an honest mistake.

"Isn't it kind of late for sucker spearing? I thought that was about a month ago. Besides, I didn't even know that spearing was legal around here."

Jesse looked at the floor. "We just went for something to do," he muttered.

Linda came around the corner with the IV stand, a liter bottle of Lactated Ringer's, and the materials necessary to start the fluids. She plugged the IV line into the bottle. I shaved the beaver's stocky front leg and scrutinized the unfortunate critter. Including the black, scaly tail, which constituted one-third of its length, the kit was about a foot long. The hind feet were webbed and considerably larger than the front. The beaver's mouth hung partly open, exposing the large incisors.

The immediate problem was shock, no doubt induced by the belly wounds and the strangulated bowel that drooped down the beaver's side.

"The only possibility of saving this animal is to do surgery—immediately. I'll build him up with fluids and other medications, but we have to work on that intestine and see what else is damaged inside." I opened the valve on the IV line to allow the Lactated Ringer's to drip faster.

"Do whatever you have to do, Dr. Foster. My mom is

worried that the DNR warden might find out and I'd be in trouble. You won't tell them, will you?" Jesse looked worried.

"No. I promise I won't tell them." Little did the boy know that I would never notify the DNR. My thoughts began to race. I had learned my lesson the hard way. Just the month before someone had brought an orphaned otter in for help. When the Department of Natural Resources found out that the otter was in my hospital, they seized it. To make matters worse, the helpless orphan was later sold to a local roadside zoo.

"Don't worry, I won't tell," I reassured him.

"My mom will be glad to hear that." He sighed in relief.

"I'm going to take the beaver back to the surgery room, but before you go, draw Linda a map of where you speared the fellow. If he gets better, we need to take him back where you found him." I knew from other experts that the colony would take this guy back, but he had to heal first. "I have fished Rocky Run for trout so I pretty much know where you're talking about."

"We speared 'im right next to the pond by the first spring hole, if that helps."

"You don't need to draw a map then. I know where that is." I turned to Linda, who was standing by me. "I'll carry the beaver. You get the IV stand."

Jesse Gatlin thanked me and left. On his way out the door I emphasized again that the DNR would not find out about the speared rodent.

The surgery was long and complicated. Two of the prongs from the spear had penetrated the beaver's body. I had to make an incision across his entire midsection to explore and clean the lesions. The blood supply to the eviscerated portion of the small intestine had been inadequate. A six-inch section of devitalized bowel had to be removed. A puncture directly into the stomach necessitated suturing. The entire abdomen had to be flushed to remove bits of hair, ingesta, and other contamination. Judging from the damage and length of time it had been since the injury, I was surprised the beaver was still alive. I was equally surprised that the little cuss made it through the ninety-minute surgery. He wanted to live!

Linda spent the next half-hour cleaning and disinfecting the beaver's fur. She finished just as our new patient began to stir.

"There, you don't smell like fish anymore," she said to the beaver and placed him on a blanket in a cage. She turned to me, "What do you think we ought to call him? He has to have a name."

I thought for a moment. We had been assigning names to wildlife patients since we started treating them. It wasn't necessarily by design or an attempt to make pets of the wild creatures. Indeed, we did everything we could to ensure that the patients were not treated like pets. After all, they would need to survive in the wild again. But giving them names didn't change the way we rehabilitated them, and sometimes it avoided confusion. Once we had three broad-winged hawks hospitalized, and individual names made it easier for us to talk about them.

"How about Kit? The young are called kits, so it's kind of appropriate." I looked at Lin for approval.

"Yeah, Kit. I like that. It has a nice sound to it. Kit," she repeated. She looked into the cage.

Kit was trying to stand. The IV line was in danger of wrapping around him.

"Lin, you'd better disconnect the line before he gets tangled in it. He's had enough fluids for now anyway." I watched as Linda carefully untaped Kit's leg. The beaver looked peculiar. Sterile surgery had required close shaving over virtually the entire abdomen. This swath had given Kit a distinctive, albeit undignified, appearance.

"Do you think he'll make it?" Linda looked concerned.

"His chances are good. He's already made it through the worst part. But I'm a little worried about the intestine. When two ends are sewn together, there's always a minor chance of leaking. We'll have to keep him off food for twenty-four hours to give the bowel a chance to seal. If he's eating by tomorrow afternoon, I'd guess he's out of the woods." I contemplated the prospects of this beaver's release. "Did you know, Lin, that an adult beaver can chew through a five-inch willow in three minutes?"

"You're kidding." Linda looked amazed.

"No, I'm not." It was hard not to admire this creature. "They even have different dam designs, depending on the speed of the current."

For the moment, there was nothing more we could do. We left Kit to recover fully from the anesthetic. By now it was nearly noon. Just enough time to complete the two scheduled spays before afternoon appointments.

The next day Linda mixed Esbilac—a commercial milk replacement for animals—with water and a tad of safflower oil. Kit drank readily, first from an eyedropper and then from a bottle. The beaver looked a little large to be on milk, but I knew that in the wild this one would still be nursing. Linda's knack for feeding orphaned mammals was not lost on Kit. Her practice with countless motherless puppies and kittens qualified her to perform this task. She was a proven mother.

By the third day, at Linda's prodding, Kit was eating commercial rodent pellets in addition to the liquid concoction. It was also on the third day that Jesse Gatlin stopped back at the hospital to visit his inadvertent victim. Jesse beamed when he saw Kit lumbering back and forth in his cage.

"Does this mean that you'll be able to let him go?" Jesse asked.

"I'd say yes. Probably in another ten days or so. I want to keep him here until I take out the stitches— possibly longer. I want to be sure he's healed. It'll also give him a chance to grow back a little hair. We had to shave a lot." I gestured toward the beaver. "See?"

"Oh, wow! You did have to shave a lot." His eyes widened. "Wait till my mom hears that you fixed 'im. She'll be happy." He paused. "My uncle is going to call you about it, too. Mom called him last night and told him the story. He said he wanted to talk to you."

"Is that right?" I hesitated. "Who's your uncle?"

"My uncle Bud, from Madison."

"Oh, from Madison?" I puzzled. "No problem. Tell him to call me at work whenever he wants."

An exuberant Jesse left after a ten-minute visit with Kit. His uncle called me later that day.

"Yes, Jesse told me you were going to call. What can I do for you?"

"I'm Bud Roland, an engineer with the Department of Transportation—the DOT—and I'm calling about the beaver you're looking after. You are the vet that worked on the beaver, aren't you?"

"Yeah, that's me." He must have been used to veterinary hospitals with more vets. I was the only one in my hospital. "I'm Dr. Foster."

"Well, I want to talk to you about that beaver. Our department gets calls every day complaining about too many beavers. They've backed up water right over the road in lots of areas. According to my friend from the DNR, the beaver population is on the upswing, and they're wreaking havoc all over."

I knew that the beaver population in the Northwoods was on the rise. Just yesterday a client had complained that beavers had gnawed a large chunk out of a birch tree by his shoreline. And I had seen new dams on streams

*The felled trees on the other side of the bay serve
as testimony that a colony of beavers reside on
this northern Wisconsin wilderness lake.*

where there had been none the year before. I still wasn't sure what Jesse's uncle really wanted, though.

"Yes, I know about the reported beaver problem. I've heard about it, read about it, and seen it myself." That ought to impress him, I thought.

"If that's the case, why are you helping one? We all know there are too many already. We don't need another." His voice started to rise.

I sensed what he was saying, but wanted to hear him verbalize it. "What exactly do you mean?"

"What I mean is, can't you put the beaver to sleep? Just tell the Gatlins that it died. That wouldn't really be dishonest."

"Of course, I can't put this one to sleep. He was brought here to be helped, and that's exactly what I'm doing." I was getting angry. Didn't this guy have anything better to do?

"It's the principle of the thing. There are too many beavers in Wisconsin. Even the DNR is pulling their hair trying to figure out what to do. I don't think they'd like it if they knew you had one."

"I took an oath in vet school, and I don't recall the DNR being mentioned in it at all. In other words, I don't answer to them." Since it had become known around the state that I took care of injured wildlife and released them back to their natural habitats, the DNR hadn't supported me. In fact, some wardens and other DNR employees had gone to great lengths to discourage my work. I thought again of the otter they'd seized the previous month.

"Don't worry," Bud said. "I won't inform the DNR. I don't want to get Jesse in trouble. I checked, and he was spearing illegally. . . . But can't you see that you shouldn't be helping the beaver?"

"No, I can't see that at all." I was sympathetic with some aspects of the problem, but there was another perspective. I didn't expect to change the mind of Mr.

Roland. But I decided to try. "You've probably already thought of this, but did you ever wonder what the building of roads did to the streams? Did you ever wonder how we affected the beavers? They were here first, you know. And if you're worried about a few trees the beavers might cut down, did you ever wonder what the Northwoods looked like when the beavers were here without man?" I didn't let him respond. I'm not sure he wanted to. "The entire North Country was virgin forest until the loggers changed all that in the last century. In fact, logging still is big business here. Not that I'm against it, but the beavers don't even compare with the logging companies."

"Well, ah . . ." He hesitated long enough for me to catch my breath and start again. I didn't consider myself an expert on beavers, but I did have more to say.

"And did you know that beaver dams are not all bad? They reduce erosion and they improve waterfowl nesting habitats. Furthermore, you ought to appreciate the part the beaver played in the history of this country. Did you know that most of North America was explored by trappers and traders in search of beaver pelts? And of course you know that some of America's greatest financial empires were founded on profits from beaver pelts—like our first millionaire. Beavers are a part of our heritage."

"Welcome to the twentieth century, Doc! That's all fine and dandy, but we're talking about progress here." He sounded annoyed and somewhat amused. "You like good roads, too, don't you? And if the beavers were chewing the trees in your front yard, wouldn't you be upset?"

"Yes, I do like good roads, and there may be isolated cases where something has to be done. As for trees in the yard, a little fencing is all that's needed to protect them. But then again, it's easier to kill the beaver, huh?" It was always ironic to me to hear people who live on lakes complain about damage. After all, a typical lakeside landscape job often necessitates the cutting of literally hundreds of trees to make room for house, garage, and manicured lawn. In many cases, less than a dozen trees are left. But when a beaver needs one of the remaining trees for food, the property owner inevitably blames the animal for destroying the shoreline. Somewhere, we've lost that perspective. Who really destroyed the shoreline?

I tried to retain my composure. I was not a defender of everything that every creature did, nor did I think of myself as a fanatical advocate of the beaver's rights. But someone had to start speaking for the animals.

"I can see I'm not going to change your mind. And now I know why they were talking about you at the DNR. Come on, now, don't you think you're being a little irrational? One little beaver won't matter!" the engineer wheedled.

Good, I thought. He had fallen into his own trap. "You're right, Mr. Roland. One little beaver won't matter at all. That's why I'm going to release him in a week or so. And I hope he eats every damn tree in sight! Goodbye." I laughed and hung up the phone.

I walked back into the kennel and stared at Kit. Awakened from his nap, he perked up his head. "Why'd you get me in all this trouble?" I whispered. I had heard most of Mr. Roland's arguments before. Obviously I knew that Kit's life was not important to the beaver population. But it was important to Linda and me. And to Jesse. Most of all, it was important to Kit.

ALL
THE QUACKS

"IS THAT A MALLARD?" LINDA PEERED INTO THE CAGE. "IT looks like the kind of duck that's often down by our dock."

"You got it. It's a mallard, all right. It came in yesterday. See what you miss when you take a day off?" Linda hated to miss out on the goings-on in the hospital, especially with wildlife, but she'd worked for two months, seven days a week, without a break. She needed a day off.

"Wilson was brought in by a couple of campers who found him along the highway up by Boulder Junction. I X-rayed him, and he's got a broken wing—otherwise okay. What do you think of the name Wilson?" I laughed a little. "Fran and Maggie stopped by yesterday and named him. It was Maggie's idea. Fran didn't like it, but I did."

I looked in at the drake mallard. He had a dark-green head with a narrow, sparkling white ring around his neck. His bill was a deep yellow, wide and flat—characteristic of the dabbler ducks. Like other dabblers, mallards eat by tipping forward in the water, their hind quarters in the air. Here in the Northwoods, they prefer seeds of sedges, pondweeds, and other aquatic plants. They also eat leaves, stems, and tubers of rooted plants and occasional aquatic insects.

Wilson's rich chestnut breast was accented by his gray body. His wings were a slightly darker shade of gray with a white-bordered, bluish-purple speculum. Standing in the cage, he had spread his toes in order to support his plump body, giving the impression that his feet were too big for him.

"He sure is a beautiful duck," Linda said admiringly. "What'd you have to do to him—just bandage his wing?"

"No, the fracture was a bad one. I had to pin the wing."

Surgery had been required to align the two segments of the broken humerus, the largest bone in the wing. I had run a stainless-steel surgical pin through the fractured bone to hold it together. Next, I had bandaged the broken wing tightly against Wilson's body. The bandage would minimize movement and ensure proper healing.

"How long will he—I mean Wilson—be here?"

"With a little luck, the bones could be healed in three weeks or so. Birds heal fast. I'll probably keep him for an extra week, just to make sure. We might have to exercise that wing as soon as the fracture is stable. I don't want the muscles to atrophy."

In his run across from Wilson's cage, Keebler, a West Highland white terrier, barked several times. Wilson stood straight up and craned his neck to see the origin of the noise. After a few seconds, satisfied he was safe, he settled into his former posture. He even grabbed a mouthful of the fresh lettuce I had offered him earlier.

"By the way, Lin, do we still have any chicken food— you know, that mash—at home? Remember, we bought some a while back for that wood duck we had?"

"Yeah, as a matter of fact, it's in the basement where you put it. Do you want me to run home and get it right now?"

"No, I gave him some birdseed we had here, and lettuce, and bread. That'll do for now. We'll bring the mash in tomorrow."

The phone rang in front. Linda darted to answer it. A new day at the animal hospital had begun. During the next five hours I saw one sick Siamese cat, two healthy black kittens that needed worming and vaccines, and one golden retriever with a sore leg. That was just for starters. A German shepherd named Max came in smacked full of porcupine quills—for the fifth time that summer. Four schnauzer neonates came in for tail docking and dewclaw removal. My last morning appointment was a liver and white springer named Jeb that had been in a dogfight. It took me nearly an hour to patch him up. Vet med was never boring.

That afternoon I glanced up at the surgery room clock. One-fifteen, exactly. I looked back down and delicately parted the tissue. Through the one-and-a-half-inch incision, I gently pushed the intestines to one side with my left forefinger. With my right hand, I inserted the spay hook deep within the yellow Lab's abdomen to secure the oviduct. Blood trickled from the wound I'd made. I withdrew the spay hook and patted dry the incision site with a gauze sponge.

"Ror, you're not going to believe this. Someone just called from Big Saint Germain Lake, and they're bringing in a duck with a fishhook stuck in it. Isn't it funny how, whenever we get a certain kind of animal, we get another right away? Look, we haven't had an injured duck in here in a month, and now we'll have two."

I looked up at Linda. Her tanned face beamed enthusiasm. She was the perfect person for her job. She radiated warmth and compassion for the animals and their owners. Clients knew it was genuine, and so did I.

"What kind of duck? Did they say?"

"All he said is that it had a brown head. I don't think he knew. What kind of duck has a brown head, anyway?"

"I'm not sure. Let me think about it for a minute." The phone rang again, and Linda departed. I finished the spay and carried the Lab back to her cage.

Less than a hour later, a retired couple arrived with the expected fowl patient. The woman waited in the reception area while Linda ushered the man into the first exam room. I followed.

"Why don't you set the box on the table?" I said to him.

He complied and I extended my hand. "Hi, I'm Dr. Rory Foster. I'm sure glad you cared enough to drive all the way from Big Saint."

The man shook my hand. "Glad to meet you. I'm Robert Webster. I read in the paper about your interest in wildlife. That's why I called you."

"Well, I'm by no means an expert, but I'll do whatever I can so this duck can be returned to your lake." I motioned to the box. "What exactly happened?" I reached over and peeled away the silver electrician's tape from the brown cardboard box.

"My neighbor left a minnow out on a bobber overnight. He apparently went to work early this morning. When I got up I noticed the duck flapping around on the water. The rod was tied to the dock."

"How'd you catch him?"

"I rowed out there and netted the poor thing." The man's short, well-trimmed gray mustache twitched nervously. His dark brows wrinkled in concern. I could tell he was upset. "The hook was way down, so I cut the line. It's still sticking out of the duck's mouth."

With both hands, I reached in and firmly grasped the unfortunate creature. The duck squirmed a bit and let out a low, unmelodious squawk when I lifted her from the box. The bright rust-brown crested head and long, red, pointed bill immediately caught my eye. The rest of the long-bodied bird was gray with a white patch on each wing. I had seen this species many times on past fishing outings.

"What kind is this, Doc?" Mr. Webster asked.

"She's a merganser—an American merganser. They're also called common mergansers." Fortunately I knew the species. I didn't know every duck of the Northwoods, but this was one of my favorites.

The fish line hung about a foot out of her beak.

"Mr. Webster, can I get you to hold her like this? Just hold the wings fairly tightly against her body and keep your face away. It's easy," I coaxed. The gentleman followed my directions and held the merganser. I pried open the red bill to locate the fish hook. My fingers felt the saw-tooth edges of the beak. The duck twisted about on the table, but I was able to calm her long enough to look deep down the throat.

"Darn," I said. "The hook is way down. I'm going to have to sedate her and take an X ray. That's the only way we'll know where it is. Why don't you leave her here and I'll call you later."

"Whatever you say, Dr. Foster. We want to do whatever is best for the duck. Do you want me to put her back in the box?"

I paused for a second. "Actually, why don't you just hold her for a minute. I'll give her a sedative so she won't hurt herself when I take the X ray." I didn't routinely sedate all birds that needed X rays, but because the duck appeared agitated, I knew I should this time. Besides that, the sharp, loonlike bill looked as if it could be dangerous.

Robert Webster looked a bit worried but did comply with my request. The anesthetic worked within a minute or two, and he left. I said I would call him later that day. He promised he would talk to his neighbor about leaving unattended fishing lines out overnight.

The radiographs revealed the hook to be halfway down the neck, about where the rust plumage met the gray. I gave the merganser another dose of the sedative, enough to completely anesthetize her. Linda carried the duck into the surgery room while I set about finding the equipment I would need.

I held the film up to the lighted X-ray viewer to determine exactly where the fishhook was lodged. "Linda, pluck a one-inch square from the left side of the neck just below the rust color."

My method of removing fishhooks of this sort was to push the hook through the esophagus and skin, clip the barb and then pull the line. This procedure allows for fairly easy removal with minimal tissue damage. The only thing I had to be sure of was not to hit the major vessels or nerves of the neck when I pushed the sharp point of the hook through to the outside.

Linda did as I requested and lightly sprayed the skin with Betadine, a surgical prep solution. "W.G.'s ready anytime you are," Linda offered.

I slipped on my surgical gloves, ready to proceed. "W.G., what do you mean W.G.? What kind of a name is that?"

"Well, look at the feathers on the back of her head." Linda pointed to the notchlike crest, a characteristic of mergansers. "See how ragged and wild they look? I named her Wild Girl."

"Very funny. Did you ever look at the back of your head in the morning, Wild Woman? I think I'll call you W.W., then." I couldn't help my grin.

"Real cute. That's real cute, Ror." Linda reached up and directed the surgery lights onto the spot she had cleaned.

Carefully, I inserted a pair of curved Kelly forceps down W.G.'s throat. Immediately I could feel metal hit metal. I could even hear it. I had found the hook. I opened the handles of the forceps and gently clamped down on what felt like the shaft of the hook. Satisfied that I had not inadvertently grabbed tissue as well, I locked the handles together.

"Cross your fingers, Wild Woman. Here goes." I directed the point of the hook toward the featherless prepped area. The skin bulged as I pressed the point upward. I pressed harder, and the point peeped through the skin. I pushed a little harder until the barb came through.

"Fantastic," I muttered to myself. I placed the wire cutters next to the skin and began to squeeze. "Cover your eyes, Lin, or look the other way." I knew that when I cut through, the point might fly in any direction.

I squeezed harder, and with a sudden jolt the hook snapped. I heard the tip hit the wall behind Linda.

"Lin, grab the line and gently pull it. The remaining part of the hook should pull right out."

Linda did, and the shaft of the hook came out easily. She raised the line, and the cut-off fishhook dangled below. I gave the duck an antibiotic injection to prevent infection.

"Do you think she'll be okay?" Linda asked.

"Depends. If her esophagus was not too badly damaged from struggling to get free, she should heal fine. We'll know in just a day or two."

I wrapped W.G. in a blanket to keep her from flapping about until she woke up, and placed her in a cage beside Wilson. Linda studied the two ducks.

"They are both ducks, but they're certainly different. Look at the difference in the bills." She pointed at one, then the other.

"That's because each feeds on different things. Wilson is a vegetarian for the most part. His bill is made for scooping. W.G., on the other hand, is a merganser, which means 'fish duck.' Her bill is designed for catching fish." I hesitated, then added, "Come on, let's turn the light out and leave. Animals seem to wake up more smoothly in the dark."

Linda and I left the kennel just in time to start the

afternoon appointments. Things sailed along uneventfully until four-thirty. I had a minute between clients and had ventured into the kennel to make sure W.G. was still doing well. I hadn't been there long when Linda interrupted.

"There's a college student up front who wants to talk to you. Her name is Connie Hastings. She's majoring in wildlife ecology or biology and wants to work with you on wildlife. She even said she'd volunteer."

"You know, Lin, maybe we could use someone. It's getting harder and harder to properly take care of the dogs, cats, and all the wildlife, too. We spend at least eleven or twelve hours in here every day."

"Well, why don't you talk to her? She's from Stevens Point."

"Okay," I agreed. I had twenty minutes before my next canine patient. "I'd like to talk to her. Just show her to the prep room."

In a moment Linda led Connie back. Connie had shoulder-length black hair that flipped slightly upward at the ends. Her nose was a bit too wide for her slender, bronze-colored face. Her green barrette matched her deep-set green eyes.

"I'm Connie Hastings." She spoke before I could and extended her hand.

"Rory Foster," I replied politely. We shook hands.

For the next fifteen minutes I answered her questions and explained the wildlife aspect of our practice. It turned out that she was going to be a senior at the University of Wisconsin–Stevens Point, majoring in wildlife biology. She wanted to work with me for the last month of the summer in order to add to her experience and résumé.

Linda and I really did need help, and I particularly liked to help out college students whenever possible. Maybe she could work here, I thought. It'd be good for us and for her, too. One problem: I wasn't sure I liked her. She seemed a little too pushy and pretended to know too much. I'd think about it a few more minutes before offering.

"By the way, speaking of wildlife, come back to the kennel and I'll show you our patients." I started toward the kennel door.

"What do you have back there?" Her curiosity was aroused.

"You tell me." I thought I'd see if she really knew as much as she let on.

She looked into the first cage and immediately identified the mallard. Next, for a few seconds she studied the cage that contained W.G., our common merganser.

"This one's easy, too," she proclaimed. "I can tell by the head color that it's a canvasback." She was so confident in her answer that, if I hadn't known better, I would have believed her.

"Well, that's close, but she's a merganser—a common merganser. They're also called American mergansers." I didn't say it snidely. Most people probably couldn't identify this duck. I felt triumphant. She didn't know everything.

Connie looked back at Wilson, the mallard. "I know this species real well. I spent last fall helping a grad student with mallards. He was involved with a research project at the Horicon Marsh. I just helped him, but I think he got his master's degree out of it."

I glanced over at her. I could tell she wanted to explain further—to be the instructor. "What kind of research?" I bit.

"It was a two-year project to determine what happens to crippled ducks. You know, like ducks that might be crippled from gunshots. We broke the wings of over a hundred mallards, placed radio backpacks on them, and then released them into the marsh. That way we could track them to see what happened. For our controls, we broke the wings of some ducks and kept them in a pen."

It had been a fairly good day so far. I sensed it was

about to be ruined. "Let me make sure I have this straight," I said as professionally as possible. I didn't want to let on that I didn't approve. She might not tell me more. "You and a grad student intentionally broke the wings of over a hundred mallards to determine what happens to ducks in the wild that end up with broken wings during hunting season?"

"That's it, exactly," she smiled. "Statistics show that as many as three million ducks are crippled by hunters each season, and the study was designed to determine the fate of a crippled duck in the wild."

"How do you know that ducks injured by hunters all suffer from a broken wing? Wouldn't there be a lot of other injuries, too?"

"I'm sure there are," she agreed. "But a hundred things could happen. We couldn't study them all."

I didn't want to tip her off yet. I still wanted to hear more. It was obvious to me, though, that the research was practically meaningless. Certainly all ducks hit by shot don't have broken bones in their wings. So their study really didn't represent the population they claimed.

Besides, virtually anyone with an ounce of common sense could tell what would happen to a broken-winged duck in the wild. It certainly didn't take two years' worth of research and the needless suffering of over a hundred mallards. I could feel my blood pressure beginning to rise.

"Connie, isn't it rather obvious what happens to ducks with broken wings in the Horicon Marsh? After all, they can't fly. Even if they managed to dodge predators, the marsh freezes not long after hunting season." I hated research like this. Animals suffer to prove exactly what? Absolutely nothing that isn't already known.

"Well, the study showed that cripples are pretty much a total loss. Some starved. Some were killed by predators.

Others lasted until the marsh froze and then died of exposure."

Surprise, surprise. I had heard enough. The research not only inflicted needless suffering but was as unscientific as any I had ever heard. It certainly didn't say much for the great University of Wisconsin system. How could they sanction such empty "research" and even think of giving credit toward a degree?

I knew, too, that this project could not have been done without the consent of the Wisconsin Department of Natural Resources and the U.S. Fish and Wildlife Service. Their consent reinforced my opinion of both agencies.

Most of all, it said even less for the individuals involved. It was always hard for me to accept senseless cruelty toward animals. This study was atrocious. Sadly, such needless research is perpetuated by many individuals, high schools, and universities around the country.

I stared at the two ducks. Helping them would not make up for the widespread intentional cruelty toward animals, but it was something. Maybe one day others would feel the kinship with animals that Linda and I felt.

I turned to exit the kennel, a signal for Connie to follow. We walked up front.

"We're just not busy enough to warrant taking on any additional help," I said matter-of-factly.

Connie left. She must have known I was displeased. Perhaps seeing what I was doing to save two ducks would cause her to rethink the nature of that research project. Wilson and W.G. had served a greater purpose today.

I continued with the late-afternoon appointments. The more I thought about the mallard research, the more disgusted I became. Just to prove to myself that I was right, I cornered Linda in the pharmacy before our last appointment.

"Linda, what do you think happens to a duck with a broken wing out in the wild?" Linda had no training whatever in wildlife studies of any kind, but she did have common sense.

She shot me a puzzled look. "Well, if the duck couldn't fly it would obviously die."

"Thanks, Lin. That's all I wanted to know."

After our last appointment, Linda and I retreated to the kennel to look after and feed Wilson and W.G. I described my conversation with Connie to Linda. She was appalled.

Linda tore some fresh lettuce for Wilson and changed his water dish. I filled his bowl with a good supply of birdseed. W.G. was alert and appeared to be resting comfortably after her surgery. She wasn't quite ready to eat yet. I'd give the esophagus a chance to seal first. Maybe some minnows tomorrow.

As we worked with the ducks, I couldn't help but think about Connie and the research.

"This whole thing could put me in a foul mood," I said to Lin.

"Do you mean F-O-W-L or F-O-U-L?" She smiled and grabbed my arm. I could see the twinkle in her blue eyes.

I thought for a second. "Both, Wild Woman. I mean both." I squeezed her hand. I felt better.

KATIE

KATIE, A YELLOW LAB, STOOD ON THREE LEGS IN THE MIDDLE of the exam room. She carried her right rear leg completely off the floor. The dog's owner, David G. Allenduhl, sat behind Katie.

"She jumped out of the back of my pickup." Mr. Allendahl was perturbed. "Dumb dog."

I avoided the man's gaze. I had seen numerous dogs injured the same way. Even dogs that had ridden in the back of trucks for years occasionally surprised their owners. All it took was the right visual stimulus at the wrong time—a barking dog alongside the road, a scampering squirrel, or maybe a fleeing cat.

"How long ago did it happen?" I stepped toward the Labrador. Katie was a friendly dog. I lifted her upper lip. "Gums are nice and pink. Probably no internal injuries," I thought aloud. Checking the color of an injured dog's gums is a good way to determine the dog's overall condition. Lowered blood pressure, a sign of internal damage or blood loss, is manifested by pale gums. That's why the first thing nearly any vet does when examining an animal is to look in the mouth.

"It happened last night, about dark," Katie's owner confessed. "She didn't look that bad, so we waited until today." Known around town simply as D.G., Mr. Allendahl was the flamboyant type. Maybe that's what it took to succeed as a businessman on Chicago's north side, D.G.'s former domain. I hadn't talked to anyone in Minocqua who knew what he did down there, but he had money— or at least that's what everyone thought. He had moved to the Northwoods the year before, about the same time I had.

Very gently, I palpated Katie's leg. There was a definite swelling around the front of the knee. When I bent the joint, the dog flinched. "There is a knee injury for sure." I glanced at D.G. His hazel eyes were focused on a framed photograph of Linda and a fawn, Faline, that hung on the wall behind me. I couldn't describe it, but I didn't like the way he looked at the picture of my wife. For a split second, I bristled inside.

Mr. Allendahl didn't comment, so I continued my exam of the sore leg. Katie flinched again when I manipulated her hip. The ball of the femur rocked against the pelvic bone when I raised her leg. It was not in the socket. "The hip joint is dislocated, too," I said louder. "The best thing would be to take an X ray to be sure there isn't a fracture up there." I stood up and backed away from Katie. "Do you want to wait here till I get some X rays or do you want me to call you? It'll take about twenty minutes."

"How much is all this going to set me back?" D.G. looked at his watch. "Will Katie's leg be perfectly normal?" With his gray pinstripe suit and carefully combed salt-and-pepper hair, I had to admit the man looked impressive. A large diamond set in a gold ring was prominently displayed on his right hand.

My experience led me to believe that Mr. Allendahl really did not want to know what it would cost to repair

Katie's leg. And he wasn't that interested in the healing process. His questions were merely formalities. They had to be asked. That's how he would justify the decision that he had already made.

"Well, I'm not exactly sure what's wrong with her knee. While she's sedated for the X ray, I can examine it further. It hurts her too much now." I started calculating. "Without knowing the extent of the knee injury, it's hard to give you an exact figure." I paused. "The hip might pop right back in. You never know. But if the knee ligaments are torn, surgery would be required. So at this point, about the best I could do is tell you that, counting the X rays, it might cost anywhere from seventy-five to a couple hundred dollars." I hesitated. "Again, it's hard to give an accurate prognosis. With any serious knee or hip injury, there could always be a little permanent stiffness. Just like in humans."

"Oh, jeez, I don't know, Doc. Seems like a lot of money. . . ." D.G. was calculating—but not with numbers.

There are two kinds of clients who refuse proper medical treatment for their pets: those who genuinely do not have the financial resources to afford care and those who do have the money but won't spend it on their dog or cat. It is the individuals in the latter category that most irritate me.

Of course, the D.G.'s of the world rarely admitted to their lack of responsibility. Rather, as in this case, they subtly blame the veterinarian—always mentioning the money and the alleged high cost. It was all a ploy to pass the guilt. Whenever I detected this maneuver, I shoved it back. I wanted the owner to know that I knew.

"Listen, don't worry about the cost. As far as I'm concerned, you could pay five dollars a month." I knew very well that D.G. would refuse my offer. He simply did not want to spend any money on his dog.

"Well, I don't know . . ." D.G. fumbled for the words.

I knew he'd think up another excuse. Sure enough, he did. "I really don't spend that much time with the dog. Besides, you said yourself the leg might be stiff. That wouldn't really be fair to the dog." D.G. glanced at Katie. She wagged her tail. "How much would it be just to put Katie to sleep?"

Finally D.G. had said it. He had decided on that option long before he got to my hospital. That's why he hadn't called the previous evening when the accident happened.

I could respect the fact that Mr. Allendahl did not want Katie. Certainly dogs are acquired for many different reasons, and mistakes are made. But I was appalled at the number of owners who tried to solve their unwanted-pet problem by killing the animal. Just the month before, a woman who was moving to an apartment called the clinic. Because the apartment owner didn't allow pets, she requested that her healthy six-year-old dachshund be euthanized. When Linda suggested that she try to find a new home for her dog, the woman became very indignant. "That wouldn't be right," she yelled at my wife. "Schatzie wouldn't like that. She has always been with me." That type of thinking drove Linda and me wild.

I looked at Katie. The faithful canine was staring at her master. Her amber ears perked attentively. The tip of her tail flicked back and forth. Mr. Allendahl's indifference didn't change anything. The dog loved the man. There was total devotion in Katie's brown eyes. Here stood a creature that would willingly protect her owner with no regard for her own life. Despite that, D.G. was about to throw her away like an unwanted item of clothing.

I knew immediately that euthanasia was totally out of the question. This dog could be helped.

The dilemma of what to do with an injured dog that the owner no longer wants is a tough one in veterinary medicine. I disagree with vets who are quick to administer a lethal dose. After all, even if Katie's knee was damaged, both knee and hip could be fixed in just ninety minutes. Was my time so precious that I couldn't spend an hour and a half on this beautiful Labrador so she might live another dozen or so years?

"Would you mind if I fixed her and found a new home for her?" I probed. I tried to be as diplomatic as possible. I had gotten in trouble with owners in the past by skirting the euthanasia issue. Recently, in a similar situation, an Old English sheepdog with a broken leg had been brought to me. I knew the owners. They could have afforded the modest cost. I even offered a long-term payment plan. Still they refused to pay for repair of the fracture. They agreed, however, that I could find a new home for the dog. So I went ahead and did the surgery.

While the dog was recovering in the hospital, the owners had a change of heart. After all, they insisted, since I had fixed the dog's leg anyway and was trying to find a home, why not simply give it back to them? They still refused to pay for the surgery, but a new owner would not pay either, they complained. Actually, there was a certain logic to their argument.

But I wouldn't give in to them. A week earlier they would have put the dog to sleep. As far as I was concerned, they had violated a sacred contract that pets have with their owners.

"Fix her? . . . Free? . . . And find another home?" Mr. Allendahl sounded amused. "Do whatever you want, Doc." The man was condescending. "You're doing this because you need the practice, right?" he added and grinned.

I didn't answer his last question. In fact, I didn't explain my motives at all.

Abruptly and without so much as a farewell salute to

his companion, David G. Allendahl left the exam room. Katie tried to follow. She whimpered softly when the door closed in her face.

"C'mon, Katie. You're staying here." I knelt down and patted her head.

Katie, five years old in this photo, and her owner, the author, take a break from a summertime woodland hike.

BIOLOGY
NOTES

I PULLED OFF ONTO THE SHOULDER OF THE HIGHWAY, JUST past the turnoff to the Allequash Lake boat landing. I looked in my mirror. Nothing coming. No oncoming traffic either. I completed my U-turn.

Back about a hundred yards, I pulled off again. This time I got out and walked over to the dead animal. I had thought it was a dog when I first glimpsed it from my car window. Then I realized it was a wild cousin of the dog— a coyote. I had seen hundreds of carcasses along the highways, but never a wild canid. Coyotes are normally too sly to be hit by cars. My curiosity was aroused. Why had this one been hit?

I cautiously nudged the animal's denuded flank with my foot. No movement. The clump of reddish-gray fur lay beside him. The coyote's open eyes were dilated and fixed. Blood dripped from his nose. I grabbed the foreleg and gently lifted. The coyote was still limp—no rigor mortis, yet. This animal had died only minutes before. I looked at my watch: 10:23 A.M. Rather late in the day for a nocturnal creature to be roaming, I thought. Could he have been sick?

I carried the deceased canine back to the Bronco. I used a syringe from my emergency kit to draw a blood sample from the coyote's heart. This unclotted blood could still be used for some lab tests. From these tests or from an autopsy, I was hoping to learn why this one had been killed on the highway. My Sunday fishing trip could wait.

In fifteen minutes I was back at my hospital. I placed the coyote on the exam table and went into the lab. I spun 10 cc's of the whole blood in the centrifuge. This would give me enough serum to evaluate the coyote's organs. Once refrigerated, the serum would be safe until Monday. With the last cc of blood I decided to do a routine heartworm check. I mixed the blood with a special lysing agent to destroy all of the red blood cells. The solution would then be pushed through a millipore filter. If the coyote had heartworm, I would see the squiggling micro-filariae through the microscope.

I placed the membranous filter on a glass slide and peered through the binocular scope. In numerous spots, the few remaining undamaged red blood cells were agi-tating violently. I focused and there they were—micro-scopic worms called microfilariae. There were nine in the field. There must have been over a hundred on the entire filter. This coyote had heartworm.

My discovery did not have major consequences for Wisconsin wildlife management. The Department of Nat-ural Resources had reported heartworm in coyotes the year before. But if there were enough adult worms in this coyote's heart, they might have caused him to become ill. That could explain the accident.

There are many organisms that cause diseases in animals. I had learned all about bacteria, fungi, and viruses in college, but those organisms were abstract to me. Sure, with the right stains they become visible under the micro-scope's highest powers. But still, they were little more than specks. It was difficult for me to imagine their lives.

Parasites are different. You don't need an imagination for most. You can see them and feel them. They are fascinating.

The canine heartworm is one of the most important parasites in North America. Adult worms look like pieces of spaghetti and may grow to lengths of up to one foot. As the name implies, this creature lives in the patient's heart. The heartworm enjoys a literal bloodbath with every beat. But how do they know their way around the body? What mechanism is there to direct them to the circulatory pump, and only to the right side of it, at that? How could parasites like this have evolved?

And it's easy to think of the white worms as merely a constant mass of similar tissue. But, in fact, they are highly specialized animals. They have a digestive system, excretory system, nervous system, and a well-defined reproductive system. Like higher forms of life, the male and female heartworms must mate to produce offspring. How do these sightless, speechless critters tell one another apart? Could there be primitive courting behavior going on in there?

Some time after a lovemaking fling, the offspring, called microfilariae, are born. Parental responsibility stops at birth; the tiny babies are immediately washed into the general circulatory system. They can remain alive for two years this way—just free-floating through the blood. Mosquitoes offer them their only chance at growing up. Not just any mosquito, mind you. Only certain species will do.

When an accommodating mosquito bites a dog with heartworm, the bloodsucking insect may inadvertently ingest a microfilaria. What are the chances of its being sucked up in the comparatively minuscule meal of a mosquito? Do these minute worms ever cause problems in the mosquitoes that eat them? I wonder.

The chemistry of the mosquito's body is such that the microfilaria undergoes a change. After ten days on board, the microfilaria has been altered ever so slightly. It is now a larva. This metamorphosis completed, the larva migrates from the mosquito's gut back to the salivary glands. Can the mosquito feel this?

Once tucked away in the salivary glands, the larva waits for just the right moment. The next time the mosquito bites a dog, the larve springs to action and migrates back down the mosquito's proboscis. Is the larva ever fooled? Yes, maybe. There are rare cases of heartworm in cats. Were these accidental? Can a larva distinguish a cat from a dog? Or from a coyote? Had any larvae ever entered my own arm? Since the organism cannot develop in humans, how would I ever know?

If the larva is lucky enough to escape into a suitable host, it undergoes further development. For several months it remains in the tissue near the mosquito bite. Finally, the larva is triggered to move. Via the bloodstream, the growing worm is swept to the heart. Like its mother and father, the adolescent stays in the right atrium or ventricle. In another month or two, the larva will mature into an adult. If a member of the opposite sex can be found in the surrounding blood, the cycle starts anew. If the first two or three adults happen to be male, who gets the first female? How do they decide? Or does she make the decision?

I stepped away from the microscope. The fact that such a complicated parasite life cycle could exist at all was truly flabbergasting. If every stage—microfilaria, larva, and adult—depended on the stage before it for its existence, which stage occurred first? The fact that such a complex sequence of events could occur at all seemed like a miracle. For the heartworm, I say it is.

I walked into the exam room. The mystery was not entirely solved. Heartworm disease does not always cause serious illness. A few heartworms would not have caused this coyote to behave abnormally.

Starting at the front, I counted back five rib spaces on the coyote's right side. I cut through the chest wall from the back down to the sternum. The thorax was filled with blood. The force from the automobile had evidently ruptured the lung.

The right half of the coyote's heart bulged outward. I sliced through. An interwining mass of live heartworms clogged the chambers. There had to be at least thirty, maybe more. They writhed back and forth very slowly, as if in slow motion. I wondered how they had received the news of the coyote's death and their own impending doom. What was the first signal? Was it the falling temperature of the blood or maybe the low oxygen content? Or something else?

A perfect parasite does not harm its host. These worms had violated that principle. By interfering with the workings of the heart, they had impaired circulation. This led to the coyote's fatigue and slowed reflexes. The animal had not been fast enough to dodge the car.

I stared at the moving mass of worms. Their death throes were becoming weaker and weaker. Finally, they were still. They had paid the ultimate price for their imperfection.

CRITICAL
DISTANCE

ANIMALS DON'T USUALLY SCARE ME. I'VE BEEN GROWLED AT, snarled at, snapped at, hissed at, clawed, bitten, and stabbed by my patients. But that's okay. I expect it. That's how wild animals behave.

Attacked, yes. Scared, no. At least not usually. The exception to this came in a mere nine-pound package. The beast was brought to me by Carl Endicott, a wildlife specialist with the Department of Natural Resources. It was one of the few times during those early years that the DNR and I worked together on a project. It was the perceived value of the patient that prompted the unusual cooperation.

"Dr. Foster, would you mind taking a look at a fisher for us?" Carl phoned me one December morning.

"A fisher? Where did you find that?" I knew that fishers were rare in Wisconsin. "Of course I'll look at it." Carl went on to explain that a trapped fisher had been found in the national forest a few miles from his office in Rhinelander. The steel leg-hold trap was still attached. The victim needed medical attention.

Fishers once prowled over most of Wisconsin, but the high value of their pelts led to their extirpation over fifty years ago. In 1955 the Wisconsin Conservation Department, as the DNR was then called, transplanted several fishers from the Adirondack Mountains to the Nicolet National Forest in northern Wisconsin. Because the repopulation effort was still under way, every individual was deemed important.

Carl arrived with the mammal shortly after we talked on the phone.

"I managed to get the trap off, but the leg looks pretty bad," he explained. "He's a mean one, Doc. The rascal bit me. I'd better leave him in the box till you're ready to work on him." Carl laid his thick leather gloves on top of the wooden box.

"Okay, I have two more appointments, and then I'm free for a couple hours. Why don't you wait here? I'll come back as soon as I can." I closed the door and left the two of them in the exam room. I doubted whether the fisher was as difficult to restrain as Carl had suggested. After all, I was used to handling all sorts of injured wild animals. A fisher can't be that bad, I thought.

A half-hour later I returned. "Ready," I announced.

Carl reached his gloved hand into the box. The sound effects were unexpected and gruesome. A series of loud grunts, squeals, growls, hisses, hellacious screams, and snorts blasted throughout the room. Most of the pandemonium emanated from the fisher. Some from Carl.

"How many do you have in there?" I laughed.

Carl looked up from where he was kneeling on the floor but didn't respond. His gray DNR cap had fallen off. Sweat trickled down his bald head and face and dripped off the end of his nose. His mustache quivered.

I didn't ask him again. Carl stuck his hand back in the box, and the fracas resumed. Finally, he latched on to the critter.

"There, you s.o.b., you can't get me now." Carl held the embattled fisher by the back of the neck and rear feet.

The animal was no bigger than a cat but had a slightly more elongated, furry body, like that of a mink or otter. The head was broad with a flat forehead that narrowed to a rather pointed snout. The mouth drooped open, and the eyes bulged because of Carl's unrelenting grip.

I visually examined the injured front leg. The trap had left a deep indentation just above the elbow.

"Have you got 'im?" I looked at Carl. "I need to feel the leg. To see if it's still warm."

"Go ahead. I got 'im—for the time being."

I reached out and felt the dangling foreleg. "It's cold. Everything past the trap wound is cold." I pointed to the part of the leg below the imprint. "There's nothing to do but amputate." I could tell by the color and texture of the tissue that the extremity had been frozen for a number of hours. It could not be saved.

"Whatever you gotta do. There aren't many of these out there," Carl stated. "We can't tell how well he'll do on only three legs, but he'll have a chance."

Carl maintained his grasp long enough for me to administer an intramuscular injection of anesthetic. In less than five minutes, the fisher was asleep. Carl left but promised to return in the morning to pick up the animal.

Linda monitored the gas anesthetic while I set about the unpleasant task. I have always hated amputations. They are so final. But sometimes they are necessary to save the life of the patient.

First, I shaved the dark-brown hair, from the shoulder down to the foot. The fisher's tough hide had ripped where the jaws of the trap had been. Bright red blood oozed from the torn skin above the wound. Unoxygenated purple blood seeped from the tissue below and ran into the laceration.

The paw was swollen tremendously—so much so that the skin had split between two of the toes. The freezing and thawing, combined with the tourniquetlike action of the trap, had prevented normal circulation. Fluid had built up in the foot until the skin actually ulcerated.

The bones of the elbow joint were crushed. This could have happened at the instant the powerful jaws of the steel trap snapped shut, or possibly the bones broke when the fisher flailed and tumbled violently in an attempt to escape. There was no way to tell.

The cut in the skin had exposed the muscles and tendons underneath. The large tendon that inserts on the point of the elbow had ripped completely away from the ulna. The muscles that worked the elbow were torn and shredded. They looked like so much raw hamburger packed around the bone. Strands of pulverized sinew and other inflamed tissue hung disjointedly, mauled beyond recognition. Certainly the initial clamp of the trap had not done this damage. This powerful animal had struggled frenetically.

The large vein returning blood from the leg to the heart was lacerated completely in two. The large glistening nerves that once enabled this boreal creature to leap acrobatically from one tree to another were mashed and severed. The proximal section of the main artery of the limb pumped rhythmically but to no avail. The lower section had retracted and could not be found.

It was hard to see this injury and not think about the cruelty inflicted by leg-hold traps. Are the wildlife managers right? Is trapping essential?

Trappers' associations and state wildlife agencies have maintained that trapping is necessary to harvest a perceived oversupply of some animals. "It's for their own good," we're told by the well-greased PR machines.

I always grimaced when I heard their logic. I grew up in a Michigan family that hunted and trapped. My grandfather trapped. My father trapped. I trapped. I knew dozens of trappers. *No one traps to help animals!* The notion is ludicrous. Trappers trap for sport or money, period. There is no altruistic motive.

That myth aside, some wildlife officials still insist that trapping does benefit animals. They are quick to liken bobcat or otter management to necessary deer management. "They'll starve anyway" is an oft-repeated phrase used to justify the annual deer harvest. Admittedly, there is some truth to this argument. However, otters aren't starving. Bobcats aren't starving. As far as I know, trapping either species has no beneficial effect whatever. I'm not aware of any disease, for example, that will decimate the existing otter population if "selfless" trappers don't venture forth.

The Wisconsin DNR hastens to point out that otter trapping does not adversely affect the population. Otter numbers remain about the same, they say. This is certainly not a convincing argument for trapping. After all, most wildlife species are capable of regulating their populations without trapping. Undoubtedly otters would, too. Even if they did increase, what's wrong with a few more otters?

The argument that trapping is necessary to prevent the state from being overrun with too many of a given species is simply not true. There are over four hundred species of wildlife in Wisconsin. Only about 11 percent are legally harvestable. If trapping is beneficial, why in the world aren't we harvesting the other 89 percent? Why not a season on hawks, owls, robins, chipmunks, or even chickadees? After all, trapping is supposed to be beneficial to the population.

Besides the tragic cruelty to the intended victim of trapping, there is another tragedy as well. Literally thousands upon thousands of faithful, loving dogs and cats end up each year losing a paw or leg or even dying in steel traps. Thousands more birds of all sorts—bald eagles, hawks, owls, ducks, geese—are killed or maimed each year by trappers. For these reasons, many hunters I know don't like trapping, but they rarely speak out.

The sport of trapping is impossible to justify. Even if there is some obscure benefit, the suffering that this practice inflicts on its victims simply cannot be justified. At least fifty-six countries have banned the steel leg-hold trap. Are we less humane?

"Shall I turn down the anesthetic?" Linda was watching my progress.

"Yes, all the way off." I was nearly done. The entire procedure had taken about one hour. I placed the three-legged fisher on a blanket in the recovery cage.

At seven the following morning, I bounced into the kennel to check on the wild patient and the hospitalized dogs and cats. I had just entered through the doorway when the fisher exploded. Mouth agape and teeth bared, he smashed against the front of the cage. He was trying to attack—me. I wasn't even near his cage. Snarling and spitting, he lunged repeatedly against the narrow steel bars of the cage door.

I had never witnessed such ferocity. His missing leg did not seem to slow him down.

I glanced at the locking mechanism on his door to ensure it was secure. It was. I quickly left. I sat down in the prep room to catch my breath.

Before I could collect my thoughts, Linda popped into the room.

"How's the fisher? Have you cleaned his cage yet? It's probably dirty."

I rolled my eyes. "Ah, no. But you'd better clean mine."

I recalled my zoology. I had violated the fisher's critical distance. If unable to flee, this is the distance at which an animal displays antagonistic behavior toward an enemy. I was used to caged owls, which could be approached within two or three feet before they issued a

Fishers are nearly impossible to handle in captivity. This one was accidentally trapped. His leg had to be amputated.

challenge. Or eagles and hawks, whose critical distance in captivity was only a few feet more. Even the other carnivores I had treated did not "attack" at this distance.

Fortunately, Carl Endicott arrived early in the day to spell me in the care of the fisher. I couldn't help admiring this official from the DNR. He had style—unlike his perfunctory associates I knew. Carl wanted to save the animal even though there was no guarantee it would survive in the wild.

It might be years or even decades before the DNR agreed with my point of view on trapping. But Carl Endicott did offer a ray of hope that things could change. Maybe the critical distance between the DNR and me was shrinking.

ON
BIRD WATCHING

IF I WERE GIVEN THE TASK OF SELECTING THE SEVEN WONDERS of the vertebrate world, I held the first one in my hand. The female hummingbird fluttered a bit but didn't escape. The plumage on her head and back was a metallic bronze-green, which contrasted nicely with her white throat and underparts. The wings were a brownish slate, faintly glossed with purple. The middle portion of the tail was also bronze-green. It was flanked by similarly colored feathers which were broadly tipped with white.

The ruby-throated hummingbird struggled some more and then sat on my finger. She thrust her long, slender bill upward toward the feeding jar I was holding. Her tongue flicked in and out of the spout, lapping the sweetened beef broth. The extremely long tongue of a hummingbird is split and, because of its unique anatomy, is capable of tremendous extension. A foraging hummingbird does not constantly hold its tongue in the nectar as a moth does, but rapidly inserts and withdraws it. Insects, a substantial portion of the diet, are ingested in the course of drinking the nectar. I had added beef broth to the sugar water to more closely approximate the bird's natural diet.

145

Ruby, our smallest patient ever, drank for at least five minutes, then stopped. She needed a short rest.

My new avian friend had been named by Millicent Wilder, who had brought her to the clinic earlier in the day. Fact is, Ruby was not a new name. The eccentric old lady had dubbed the bird years before.

"I know she's the same one, Doc. I've been watching Ruby for five years." She paused. "I shouldn't have enclosed that porch. The poor thing was unacquainted with the new windows."

It was difficult to argue with Millicent. She was a retired ornithology professor and Minocqua's best-known bird watcher. The eighty-four-year-old woman was often seen strolling about town or around the lakeshore in khaki walking shorts and sneakers, carrying her ever-present binoculars. She always wore one of two jackets—a green nylon windbreaker for the pleasant days, and a red and black checkered wool coat on the colder days. During extremely cold weather she remained at home and trained her spotting scope on one of her five bird feeders.

"Oh, really," I speculated and looked at the small box that housed the patient. The box flap read "Nature's Finest—Jasmine Tea." I lifted the fragile hummingbird off the bed of cotton.

"Ruby, love, you have to stay here with Dr. Rory." Millicent was talking directly to the bird. The lady's face was surprisingly wrinkle-free. Except for crow's-feet at the corners of her eyes, her golden-brown complexion belied her age. Her thinning white hair was cropped short so as not to interfere with birding.

Maybe this woman did recognize Ruby. Once I had read about a hummingbird in California that had befriended an elderly gentleman. Reliable reports had it that the bird actually accompanied the man on walks and even sat on his shoulder.

"Maybe it's not too serious," I said and smiled at this remarkable woman. I sure hoped the bird was not injured badly. There wasn't much I could do with this smallest of all Wisconsin birds. It was so tiny that normal veterinary procedures—X rays, blood tests, temperature procurement, or any meaningful exam—were exceedingly difficult.

"When Ruby is better, just let her out. She'll come home," Millicent announced confidently and left.

I wondered about that. It was about three miles to Millicent's house. Since the hummingbird spends every winter in Central America and allegedly finds her way back to the lady's place each spring, a three-mile trip from Foster Animal Hospital would be a snap.

I tipped the red solution upward so Ruby could once again drink from the spout. I tried to imagine all of the miniature parts of this bird. The heart, though extremely small, was proportionately larger than that of any other warm-blooded animal. During heavy exercise, it could beat 1,260 times per minute! That rate was necessary to operate the wings, which could beat up to 80 times per *second!* To maintain the oxygen level to do all that work, the hummingbird must breathe 300 to 400 times per minute. The body temperature averages 104 degrees.

The nourishment required to maintain this enormous metabolic rate is astounding. A hummingbird must consume 3 percent of its body weight in protein each day. This requires 650 fruit flies or a similar number of other insects. Also, the bird must eat 70 percent of its body weight in sugar every day. (By comparison, if humans required as much, we would need to consume about 100 pounds of sugar daily.) Daily water consumption for the hummingbird is four times the body weight. An equivalent amount for the average human would be 75 gallons!

One of the most remarkable features of this feathered critter is its unique flight. The wings of "hummers" act

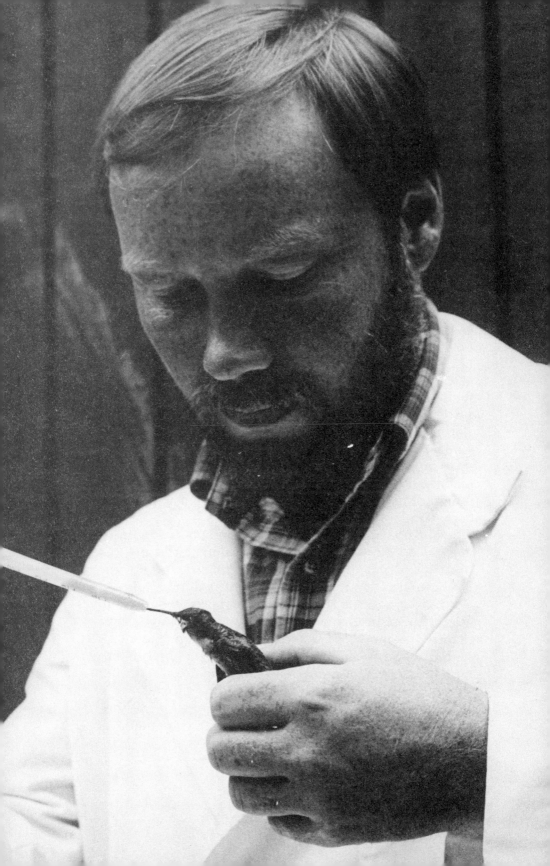

like aerial oars, the direction of which dictates the movement. Unlike other birds, hummingbirds, because of their special musculature, have as much power to move their wings upward as they do on the downstroke. This allows them to fly not only forward but also backward or simply to hover like a helicopter.

The most unique thing of all and the characteristic that makes hummers truly a wonder of the living world is their ability to conserve energy. Quite simply, the birds cannot possibly ingest enough calories during the night to maintain their exceptionally high daytime metabolic rate. To avoid burning out, most of the three hundred species of hummingbirds undergo a period of torpidity each night. It's almost like nocturnal hibernation or suspended animation. If the ambient air temperature is low, a hummingbird's temperature can drop to under fifty degrees. Respirations decrease to fewer than fifty breaths per minute, and some birds might not breathe for five minutes or longer. In this state, the metabolic rate drops to less than one-tenth the daytime rate.

In torpor, hummingbirds sit with their eyes closed, feathers fluffed, and the bill pointed straight up. If removed from their perches, they lie motionless, unable to resume their perching position. Torpid hummingbirds have been found on the ground after having been dislodged from trees by high winds at night. An apparently lifeless hummingbird thus found should not be presumed dead. Unless injured by the fall, the torpor will reverse in the morning and the bird will be able to fly away.

The author feeds an injured female ruby-throated hummingbird. These birds, the smallest in the world, are very cooperative—even friendly—in temporary captivity.

Ruby drank thirstily. She stopped again and cocked her head from side to side, eyeing her captor. Already Ruby was more alert than when Millicent dropped her off. Hopefully the hummingbird suffered nothing more than a mild head concussion. I had seen many birds injured from window collisions. Very often, if kept safely inside, away from neighborhood cats and dogs, and fed, they completely recuperate in a day's time.

Because I did not entirely understand torpidity in hummingbirds, I decided to let Ruby sleep outside. After all, she was used to the cool evening temperatures, and I didn't want to interfere with her metabolic cycle. I rigged a suitable wire birdcage for her, complete with resting branch and hummingbird feeding station. Ruby would be fine until morning.

Linda and I were excited when we left work that Friday night. We had company coming for dinner. T. J. Dunn and his family were due to arrive at our house at seven-thirty.

T.J. and I swapped practice and fishing stories until past eleven. The quiescent evening was finally shattered by a phone call at eleven-thirty. Shannon, an Irish setter, had encountered a porcupine. His owners wanted to bring him into the hospital immediately. T.J. volunteered to accompany me.

It was nearly half-past midnight, and we were still removing the tenacious quills. There had to be over a hundred. They were lodged all over Shannon's face, inside the mouth, and even in his tongue.

As I bent over the dog's head, I was struck with an idea. Maybe I should pull a prank on T.J. Certainly he would know nothing of torpidity in hummingbirds. I smiled and imagined a conversation we would have after we finished pulling the quills.

"By the way, T.J., what do you know about hummingbirds? I got one in today," I would start.

"Not much, Ror. Do you really have one here? In the hospital?" T.J. would be surprised. "I've never seen one up close." He would squint at me.

"Well, I was hoping you'd examine it for me. I can't find too much wrong. Maybe you'll notice something I've missed." I would play on his ego.

"Okay, let's have a look," T.J. would agree. I strongly suspected he knew nothing about the hummingbird's sleeping habits.

I would have him get the bird while I cleaned up the room. I would convince him to remove Ruby from the cage.

"Go ahead. Reach in there and take Ruby out," I would coax. It was a crisp June night. I knew the hummingbird would be sitting in a torpid state on a twig.

T.J. would open the cage door and carefully remove Ruby. Of course the torpid bird would fall over in his hand. That's when I'd nail him.

"T.J.," I would exclaim, "what did you do to the bird? You must have squeezed her too tightly. Look, you killed her." I would be dead serious.

His eyes would widen. I pictured him staring blankly into the palm of his hand. "But, I didn't squeeze—"

"T.J., hummingbirds are very fragile. Any pressure at all on the chest and they just die." It wasn't very often that T.J. could be so completely fooled. I wouldn't let up. He'd feel terrible. But somehow I had to get him back for the incident he pulled with Mrs. Primerose.

I chuckled to myself as I pulled the last quill from Shannon's throat. Since T.J. knew nothing of hummingbirds, my scam really wouldn't be fair. But at this point, I didn't care.

"T.J., there's a hummingbird out back if you want to see one," I offered after the canine patient left. "Why don't you go get the cage while I clean the room?" After he left, I laughed again at how I was going to get him.

Minutes later T.J. reappeared in the exam room. "Ror, I don't know how to tell you this." T.J.'s face was somber. "There's no bird out there. The cage was on the ground with the door open."

"What!" I panicked. I stared at the empty birdcage T.J. was holding. The door hung open.

"A cat took off through the woods when I opened the back door. . . ."

A sick feeling came over me. "Oh, damn," I choked. I thought about the defenseless hummingbird being eaten by a cat. I should have kept her inside. I sat down on the exam room bench and leaned over, face in my hands.

"Listen, buddy, I'm really sorry. It wasn't your fault." T.J. tried to console me.

"Yeah, but it was my fault. I put Ruby out there." I felt terrible.

T.J. began to giggle, and then belly-laugh. I looked at my former employer. He had that gleam in his eye. I'd seen it before. Right then I knew I'd been had.

"Where's the bird?" I demanded.

"Don't worry. She's safe. Come here and take a look." We started toward the back door. T.J. turned to me, grinning. "Hey, c'mon, Foster. Haven't you ever heard of torpidity? You're the wildlife doc!"

Ruby sat, sound asleep, on her perch. In her trance, T.J. had lifted the hummingbird, branch and all, out of the cage and carefully placed her on top of an old wood duck house someone had given me.

I watched as my colleague replaced Ruby in the cage. The bird remained fast asleep.

By the next morning Ruby's concussion had abated. The dainty, aerial acrobat buzzed my head once and then flew away. Amazingly enough, Ruby left in the direction of Millicent Wilder's house. This little bird would delight Millicent and T.J. for years to come.

FRAN'S
PET MOTEL

I SWUNG MY BRONCO OFF HIGHWAY 51 ONTO AIRPORT ROAD, en route to Fran's Pet Motel to check over an abandoned litter of puppies. Someone had left a cardboard box containing four beagle pups on Fran's doorstep. This sort of thing happened all the time. It was easier for me to go to Fran and Maggie's than it was for them to haul the pups to me. The orphans needed to be vaccinated and wormed. We had agreed on a noontime visit.

About a quarter-mile down the road, I pulled off to look at the eagle's nest. I chuckled when I thought about the eaglet Fran, Maggie, and I had helped the summer before. I picked up my binoculars from the seat. The nest was considerably larger than I remembered. This year's offspring sat atop the towering dead tree—one youngster directly on the nest, the other perched on one of the few remaining limbs.

I searched the surrounding sky with the binoculars. The tiny speck I had seen before turned into a mature bald eagle—one of the parents, I suspected. Its majestic wings were spread and fixed. Like a glider, the bird soared effortlessly on the wind currents high above. During the few minutes I was watching, the eagle changed altitude three times—compliments of the swirling drafts. Not once did the bird flap its mighty wings.

I pulled back onto the road and headed for the pet motel. Maggie had reported the beagle puppies to be a little thin, otherwise in good shape. Like the rest of the United States, the Northwoods suffers the consequences of dog and cat overpopulation. I hated the tragedies that inevitably occurred. According to a prominent veterinary journal, approximately 20 percent of all dogs in the United States are unnecessarily euthanized or die from a problem associated with abandonment—injury, exposure, or starvation—each year. I vowed to address that problem in a meaningful way one day. Until I thought of how to do so, I would have to be content with trying to find homes for the unwanted pets I knew and providing free care to the strays Fran and Maggie acquired.

The road took a hard jog to the right. I glanced out at the runway where the grounded loon had been rescued. It was amazing that Maggie had spotted it so far away, I thought.

A silver Suburban blocked the driveway into the pet motel, so I parked near the entrance. It was only one hundred feet or so to Fran's house anyway. I walked past Fran's orange Case tractor. A load of gravel remained in the bucket. Gravel for the dog runs, I figured.

Fran's house was on the right, Maggie's on the left. An indoor facility for the boarding dogs connected the two Wedgwood-blue abodes. Farther to the left of Maggie's house were the outdoor dog runs. There were at least a dozen runs, though an exact count was difficult from my vantage point. The enclosures were not arranged in any particular order. Rather, the yard appeared to be a hodgepodge of wire. There were different types and styles of fence all mixed together, some going this way, some that way. Only Fran and Maggie knew their way around the maze—simply because they did all the building themselves.

Interspersed throughout the kennel area were a variety of mature hardwoods. One limb of a huge maple had prematurely turned a fiery red, a certain harbinger of autumn. The scattered trees provided plenty of shade for the summer canine residents.

Above the din of the barking, I could hear Fran shouting. The owners of the car in the driveway must be picking up their dog, I thought. I stood in front of Maggie's house waiting for the dog owner to leave.

"Hi, Doc." Maggie's voice surprised me. I turned to see her standing inside her screen door.

"Hi, Maggie. Looks like someone is here to get a dog." I looked through the trees back toward the runs.

"Yeah, that's Mrs. Mortenberry. She's here to pick up Vincent, her crazy Dobe." Maggie pushed open the door. "Look what I have." Her blue eyes peered out from under the brim of her battered pith helmet.

"Where did you get that?" I asked.

Maggie grinned proudly. She was holding a young raccoon under one arm. It couldn't have weighed more than a few pounds. The furry critter squirmed and reached up toward Maggie's face with one paw. "Isn't he a cutie? This is Bonzo. We're taking care of him for some people up Boulder Junction way. He is an orphan. His mother was killed by a car." Maggie looked down at the raccoon. "His owners had to leave town for a wedding. They'll be back tomorrow."

"Bonzo, huh?" I looked at Maggie's friend. "What are they going to do with him?"

"Let him go in two weeks. They've raised 'coons before and let them go," Maggie said.

Of all the wild animals I knew, raccoons were the easiest to raise and let go again. Of course I never advised interceding unless it was certain they were orphans. Fortunately, releasing hand-raised raccoons back to the wild rarely caused problems.

"Good. These rascals can become very rambunctious as they get older. This one should be let go soon, be-fore—"

"Tell me about it," Maggie interrupted. "The little devil got away on me last night in the basement. He tore everything apart before I could catch him."

"What happened?" I knew Maggie loved to tell stories.

"The bugger escaped from his cage and ransacked my stuff. It was about one o'clock in the morning when I heard him unpacking all my boxes. I went downstairs but couldn't get close to him. Finally, I had to get a piece of chicken from the 'frigerator. I tied it to my fishing line. Each time Bonzo went for it, I reeled it in a little closer. It took darn near forty-five minutes to get the little beast back in his cage." Maggie gloated over her ingenuity. "That's why I have the leash. I'm not gonna go through that again."

I thought about Maggie in her basement rooting around among sixty-some-odd years of collectibles, in the middle of the night with a fishing pole. I laughed out loud.

Just then, Bonzo twisted and turned and flipped free of Maggie's arm. He safely landed on all fours. "There. That's why I have this." Maggie pulled on the leather leash which was attached to Bonzo's red harness.

This motherless baby raccoon assumes a defensive posture in his cage. Even though young raccoons are friendly, they can be-come destructive and dangerous when they mature. Note: *The author does not recom-mend any wild animals be kept as pets.*

"He looks pretty secure." The full harness went around the neck, encompassed both front legs and fastened around the midsection.

"Maggie, get that thing inside." Fran's head poked out of the kennel office door. "She's comin' with Vincent."

Before Maggie could move, Vincent bolted through the door Fran was holding open. Mrs. Mortenberry was unceremoniously yanked through the door. The sleek Doberman immediately saw Bonzo at Maggie's feet and bolted toward his quarry. I could see the dog's head momentarily jerk backward as he reached the end of his leash. This time Mrs. Mortenberry lost her grip, and Vincent bore down on the raccoon.

"Maggie, look out!" Fran shrieked. In that split second I glanced at Fran. The toothpick fell from her mouth.

"He'll kill 'im! He'll kill 'im! Vincent hates other animals!" Mrs. Mortenberry screamed. Her stentorian voice outranked Fran's.

Vincent was only a blur. Bits of gravel and turf flew upward. Instantaneously, the powerful Dobe was on Bonzo. Bonzo leaped backward, barely avoiding the attacker's gnashing teeth. Vincent lunged for Bonzo again. This time Maggie pulled up on the 'coon's leash to haul him clear of the dog's bite. There was no stopping the dog. Reflexively, Maggie began turning to her left. With each half-step she would jerk the leash. Bonzo stayed a breath away from certain death.

In a moment of terror, Maggie turned so fast and pulled so hard that Bonzo became airborne. Vincent now ran in circles around Maggie, leaping upward toward his prey. Maggie raised her arm and was now twirling Bonzo in the air about her head. The raccoon's feet stretched horizontally like wings on a plane. On one pass, Maggie's arm hit the side of her helmet. It crashed to the ground.

By now I had the presence of mind to grab at Vincent's leash. I stepped toward Maggie and ducked to avoid

Bonzo's overhead passes. Crouched there, I scrambled for the leash each time Vincent went by. Finally, on the fourth or fifth pass, I managed to latch on to the leash. With both hands I secured Mrs. Mortenberry's dog.

"Move back. Move back," I yelled to Maggie. I held Vincent fast, and Maggie stepped backward, somehow managing to keep Bonzo aloft. It was a bewildering scene. Even Vincent cocked his head and looked befuddled.

"How do I land 'im?" Maggie hollered. "How do I land 'im?" I hadn't thought about that. How do you land a flying raccoon?

Maggie slowed the revolutions, spinning Bonzo just fast enough to keep him off the ground. By now Fran had sprinted toward Maggie. With Bonzo going more slowly, she reached out and caught him.

"What's Bonzo doing out here? For godsakes, Maggie, I told you to get back inside with him."

Maggie staggered a bit and picked up her helmet. The breeze blew her white hair across her reddened face. She grinned sheepishly but said nothing. After Mrs. Mortenberry left with Vincent, the three of us reconstructed the near disaster. Now that everyone was safe, we saw the humor in the episode. I laughed till my sides hurt.

As I vaccinated the beagle puppies, I thought about Fran and Maggie. By taking in stray and abandoned animals, they provided a valuable service to the community. And of course their work was crucial to the helpless animals. Fran could be a bit cantankerous, and Maggie grumbled sometimes about all the work. But neither woman slowed down. They weren't made that way. If a warm heart for a cold nose was to be found in the Northwoods, it was right here.

A FIERCE
GREEN FIRE

In those days we never heard of passing up an
opportunity to kill a wolf. In a second we were
pumping lead into the pack. When our rifles were
empty, the old wolf was down and a pup was dragging
a leg into impassable slide-rocks.

We reached the old wolf in time to see a fierce green
fire dying in her eyes. I realized then, as I've known
ever since, that there was something new to me in
those eyes.
—Aldo Leopold, *A Sand County Almanac*

T.J. WALKED IN FRONT OF ME. WE WERE HIKING DOWN A
former logging road, one track long since grown over
with grasses of several types, ferns, and a sprinkling of
waist-high poplars. The narrow dirt track we were trav-
ersing had been kept free of vegetation by the comings
and goings of a variety of animals—among them deer,
snowshoe rabbit, coyote, an occasional bobcat, and the
hunters and trout fishermen who sought access to the
innermost sanctum of this stretch of wilderness in western
Oneida County.

My partner and I were going trout fishing. It was

160

rare that either of us escaped emergency duty; rarer still that the two of us escaped together. But this Saturday afternoon's excursion had been planned for some time. It had all started weeks before when I had shown T.J. my map. The map had been drawn for me by Skinner Phelps, a crusty old client of mine. I took care of his bear hounds. He had five in all—one pure-bred Plott, one black-and-tan, and three hound mixes.

During Skinner's last visit, while I sutured up his black-and-tan's lacerated pad, the two of us talked fishing. I was surprised when Skinner began telling me about his favorite trout hole. I was shocked when he volunteered to draw me a map. Old-time fishermen just don't do that. I suspected Skinner's violation of that unwritten code may have been influenced by the eighty-year-old's failing health. He had suffered a heart attack recently. Perhaps he knew he'd never again be able to hike the two rugged miles to the stream. He wanted to hand down his fishing secret to somebody.

Age was finally taking its toll on the old hunter. Skinner's right hand, the middle two fingers of which were stubbed back to the first knuckle, shook terribly as he sketched a map into a distant part of Moose Skin Creek. For the most part, the trembling stopped each time the man pressed pencil to paper. A liver spot, at least one inch in diameter, lay smack in the middle of the back of his hand. Large gnarly veins bulged beneath the leathery skin.

It took Skinner nearly fifteen minutes to draw the map. The finished work resembled a treasure map. The drawing was complete with the customary landmarks. There was, of course, a dotted line to depict the path I was to take. I was to follow the logging trail for about a mile and then turn due west down a high ridge. Skinner called it Hogsback Ridge. "You'll know it's the right one," Skinner had said, "by the dead tree full of woodpecker holes just to the left of the logging trail." Hogsback was marked on the map with little jagged lines.

Two hundred paces down the ridge was a small clearing, represented by a circle on Skinner's map. From there I was to look southwest across a bog to an abandoned trapper's shack—a box on the map with a triangle for a roof. The shack was on the north shore of a small lake. Skinner had labeled this East Bear Lake. From the trapper's cabin, the path to the fishing hole led along the eastern shoreline of East Bear across a beaver dam that spanned Bear Creek. A series of what appeared to be sticks signified the dam. Once across the dam, I was to walk along the creek about eighty paces through a blueberry patch until I saw a boulder in the middle of the stream. The boulder supposedly resembled a bear's head. According to Skinner, that's how the creek got its name. Skinner had drawn what appeared to be an aerial view of a bear's head to indicate the boulder. From there I was to veer ninety degrees to the right and walk due south through a grove of birch trees. When I came to the end of the grove, I was to look west again, across a dried-up lake. A towering white pine should now be visible on the skyline. What Skinner referred to as Moose Springs lay in a hollow just beyond the pine tree. The old man assured me that once I reached the white pine, I would be able to hear the bubbling springs. A large X marked the spot. Brook trout that had never seen a fishing lure were as "thick as wood ticks on a hound's back."

Very carefully Skinner Phelps folded the map and handed it to me. "Don't get lost in the puckerbrush back there, sonny. You might not come out." He grinned widely. His bottom teeth were brown and yellow from years of chewing tobacco. There was only one tooth visible on top. That was colored, too, but not as dark. Tobacco-stained saliva dribbled out onto his lower lip. The grizzled bear hunter wiped off the brown juice with the back of his hand. A scratching sound could be heard as his hand rubbed across his stubbly chin.

Ahead of me on the path, T.J. stopped momentarily. "Let me see that map again," he requested.

I dug into my rear jeans pocket. I unfolded Skinner's map and handed it to T.J. "How many times do you need to look at it, anyway?" I joked. T.J. had studied the map many times since I had shown it to him a month ago, including all thirty-five minutes in the Bronco on the way here.

There was no doubt that Skinner's map held a certain fascination for T.J. His eyes had lit up like a ten-year-old's when I had first described it to him. We were in my clinic at the time. He practically begged me to go home and get the map. I finally relented.

When he saw it firsthand, T.J. became the ten-year-old. He was instantly entranced by Skinner's handiwork. He scrutinized the map over and over, asking me all kinds of questions about Skinner Phelps. In his imagination, the map took on a mysterious aura, almost as if its author were a high-seas buccaneer. Twice I had to remind him that the X was simply Skinner's designation for a trout-fishing spot not the buried booty of a ransacked Spanish galleon. I'm not sure I got through to him. I was convinced that T.J.'s interest in the adventure had nothing whatever to do with fishing. The allure of the map beckoned to the adventurer.

"In about another quarter-mile, we should come to Hogsback. Keep watching for the woodpecker tree. It'll be on our left," T.J. instructed. There was a seriousness in his voice. Of course I knew the marker tree would be on our left. I had gotten up in the middle of the first night after I had acquired the map and committed it to memory. I never told Linda. Certainly not T.J.

T.J. neatly refolded the map and pushed it into his faded jeans pocket. He turned and continued down the path. There was an exuberance to his step. The sleeves of his light-blue shirt were rolled up past the elbows. This gave him the look of a man about to tackle a serious job. But the shirt's untucked tail, which had caught in his rear pocket when he placed the map there, belied that appearance.

A swarm of seven or eight deerflies buzzed about him. His dark-blue baseball cap emblazoned with orange letters that read ILLINI—his alma mater—protected his head. Mosquitoes were warded off with liberal amounts of repellent. Even though they rarely lit, they still posed a nuisance. Now and again T.J. would wave his right hand in front of his face. In his left, he clutched an ultralight fishing rod, the compact kind made for backpacking.

A little farther along, the path narrowed. It was in danger of slowly being swallowed up by the adjacent forest. Loggers had left decades before and had not returned.

The prevailing trees on both sides of the trail were fir, red maple, white pine, spruce, birch, and an occasional cedar. Of all the trees, the fir was the darkest hue of green. From a distance, their tall spires looked almost black.

The herbaceous layer of the forest was a veritable botanical garden—wild sarsaparilla, starflowers, orchis, and various kinds of baneberry and violets. Considering the competition from the massive trees above, it was a wonder that the floor of the woods harbored so many species. For the most part, the plants beneath thrived because of an evolutionary trick. They accomplished their reproduction early in the year, before the leaves of the deciduous forest overhead appeared and effectively shaded them.

The logging trail had slashed directly through the otherwise dense woods, creating still another garden. The opening, even in summer, allowed just enough sunlight to permit more lower shrubs and plants to flourish. Patches of wood sorrel, Solomon's seal, nightshade, and an occasional lady's slipper encroached on our walkway.

T.J. stopped again and extracted the map from his back pocket. I pulled up alongside. "Let's see where we're at now," T.J. said.

"We're probably about three minutes farther than we were the last time you stopped." I laughed. "T.J., all we have to do is watch for the woodpecker tree opposite the ridge. Then we turn off."

"Yeah, but what if the tree blew down? What if we miss it?"

We didn't. The dead, twisted maple tree stood like an old sentry atop the next ridge. Holes shaped like goose eggs riddled its smooth gray trunk. Hundreds of trilliums surrounded its base and continued into the woods beyond.

T.J. and I turned west, down Hogsback, into a predominantly oak and maple forest. A startled raven announced our arrival. The clearing, from which point we were to see the cabin, was exactly where Skinner had said it would be.

With map in hand, T.J. directed his gaze southwest, across the spruce bog. "I see the lake but can't make out the cabin. Maybe it's been grown over since your friend was back here." T.J. looked down at the map. "This has to be right."

I agreed. There was no way we could have taken a wrong turn. After all, we had only made one. The lush summertime foliage must have been obscuring the shack.

We hiked around the bog as Skinner had directed. We were close to the shoreline of East Bear before the cabin finally emerged from the alder thicket. The trapper's shack was small, with weathered gray vertical boards for siding. A wolf skull, bleached white by years of rain and sun, was nailed beside the broken-out front window. A few patches of tar paper still clung to the peaked roof.

The partially open wooden door hung on only one rusty hinge, practically inviting us inside.

The door creaked when T.J. opened it a little wider. The initials E.P. were carved into the center panel of the door. T.J. took a tentative forward step.

"Come on, T.J., go on inside," I prodded. "What are you afraid of?"

"Nothin', oh, nothin'." T.J. crept farther inside.

I followed. A dilapidated wooden bed was built into the wall under the lakeside window. An antiquated ladderback chair, its seat missing, lay on its side in one corner. A stovepipe hole gaped through to the outside above the chair. I tried to imagine what life must have been like for the trappers who used this overnight shelter on their trapline journeys. Those days were gone.

"Hey, Ror, look at this." T.J. was pointing to a tattered brown newspaper article nailed to the wall.

The clipping was from a newspaper based in a small burg in the next county. The *Phillips Monitor*, dated November 2, 1954, had contained a picture of two trappers. The caption read: "Area trappers, Walt Boothager and Elmer 'Skinner' Phelps, proudly display their day's catch." I squinted at the faded picture. Between the two men, three wolves hung on a pole.

"You know what, T.J., this has to be Skinner's cabin." I pointed to the clipping and then to the door. "E.P., Elmer Phelps."

T.J. nodded but continued to study the photograph. "I've read that there are several wolf packs still in Wisconsin. You know, I think one of those packs lives right around here. There are supposed to be four or five in the pack."

Shortly, we left the cabin to continue our trek. I thought about the wolf skull nailed to Skinner's cabin and about the picture of the two trappers and their "catch." And I knew T.J. was correct about a wolf pack in this vicinity. I had read the reports and had seen it on the news. This area of Oneida County was one of the few in the state selected by the DNR for reestablishment of a breeding population.

Of course, this entire project would not be necessary if only the DNR, called the Wisconsin Conservation Department back then, had performed its job responsibly. The wolves' extirpation was accomplished, in large part, because the state paid a bounty on every dead timber wolf. Not only were wolfers motivated by the money but they also felt they were doing Wisconsinites a favor. After all, wolves were nothing more than vermin. Why else would the animal have a price on its head?

But wildlife biologists had changed their thinking in recent years. The folklore had been wrong. Wolves, it turns out, are not the villains people once thought. That's not to say that the animal doesn't occasionally cause problems. Anytime two predators—like people and wolves—live together there is bound to be competition. In Wisconsin, the competition was for livestock and deer. But this sort of conflict should have been dealt with on an individual basis, not by eliminating the entire population.

Just how the concern for the wolf surfaced after years of rankled emotions is hard to say. The movement was born in the late sixties. That's when the public rekindled its fascination with wildlife and wilderness.

Ecologists had answered all the pertinent questions. The wolf could be an important mechanism within wild animal populations. We're told they cull the diseased, the weak, the old. Wisconsin wolves eat deer, beaver, rabbit, mice, bugs, berries, and mushrooms. Omit one or two of those and the diet could be ours.

Like us, wolves are highly social creatures. The pack, or extended family, of two to thirteen works under the guidance of one dominant member, usually male.

Wolves mate for life, enjoy a childhood, map their

territory, like to wander and explore, may adopt orphans, teach and discipline their young, practice birth control, grow tired of their home and move on, and are intensely loyal to other members of their group. Admirable human traits, all.

If wolves are to once again survive in Wisconsin, man will have to give quarter. When a reintroduction plan was implemented in Upper Michigan a few years before, hunters illegally shot three of the four transplanted wolves.

Before I realized it, we had arrived at the beaver dam. Walking across it posed no problems at all. From there we turned downstream. It was there in the soft mud among the blueberry bushes that I spotted the track. It was like a dog's but larger—much larger. It had to be at least four and one-half inches long.

"Wolf," I said quietly to my fishing partner. I pointed to the ground. A chill went through my body. My pulse quickened. I glanced nervously at the surrounding woods.

Sure, I had known there were wolves somewhere in this part of the county. I hadn't realized they would be right here—where I was.

Of course I had studied wolves. I knew their physiology, their behavior. And I knew them to be perfectly harmless to man. But my knowledge was purely abstract, my learning from books. The track in the mud had given me a new perspective. Wolves were no longer a mere romantic notion. They were here.

But that still didn't explain my initial reaction to seeing the track. Why had I momentarily stiffened? Why had my heart rate increased? There was an indescribable energy about that track. I could feel it. I looked at T.J. He felt it, too.

I gazed back down at the track in the mud. In my mind I could almost see the owner of that pawprint, and I could imagine the scene.

The track must have been made sometime after dark the night before. The wolf had approached the stream from the south. The smell that had probably alerted his hunting senses was beaver.

By the time he reached the edge of the blueberry bushes, the beaver odor was strong. No longer shielded by trees, the wolf crouched low and crept forward toward the poplars that lined the edge of Bear Creek.

The wolf stopped again. His probing nose now told him that there were two distinctly different beaver smells. His ears perked up. He could hear the gnawing sounds of teeth on tree.

He moved forward again, bellying his way among the bushes. The pungent beaver odor became overpowering. The hunter knew that he must now find his quarry with his eyes. He peered through the leaves and carefully searched every rock, every stump and every shadow. Finally he saw his potential meal.

There were two beaver—a large adult accompanied by a kit. They were posed back-to-back, each working on his own tree. The wolf had not made a sound but something alerted the older beaver. He sat high, then turned toward the water. The kit knew enough to follow his parent.

The wolf exploded. Digging in with his oversized paws, he launched toward the kit. But he was a split second too late. The young beaver dived into the water. The gnashing teeth missed flesh. The evening's hunt would have to be continued.

"Ror, do you think we can cross the lake bed? Or, will we have to go around the end like it says here on the map?" T.J. nudged my arm and pointed to the map. I let go of my imagination.

We left the wolf track and proceeded through the wild blueberries until we were adjacent to the rock in the middle of the stream. From there we turned and passed through the birches until we could see the tall pine Skinner had described. Because the lake bed was marshy, we followed Skinner's advice and went around the south end. By the time we actually wet a line in Moose Springs, T.J. had perused the map not less than three more times since we left the wolf track.

We had great trout fishing that summer day in the North Country. I chuckled each time T.J. fumbled with the map. But the most vivid memory I have of that afternoon is still of the wolf print pressed into the mud alongside Bear Creek. It's heartening to know that the fierce green fire is still smoldering in Wisconsin. T.J. kept my map, but I'll have my first wolf track forever.

GRIZZLY

JUNE WAS THE MONTH FOR ORPHANS OF THE WILD. MY POLICY was strict. No baby wild animal would be accepted at the hospital unless there was positive evidence that the creature was indeed an orphan. Despite modern veterinary medicine and all the trappings for raising neonates—electronic diagnostic equipment, fancy incubators complete with oxygen and humidity control, and exacting pediatric animal formulas—Linda and I were still no match for natural parents. Thousands or even millions of years of parental success simply could not be duplicated in an animal hospital.

Certainly we tried and often succeeded. But there were failures, too. I can never forget the kingfisher we raised—or almost raised. The fledgling's mother had been killed by a thoughtless twelve-year-old with a BB gun. I don't know how many hours Linda and I spent shoving food down the little bird's gullet. For over a week we took turns feeding pieces of minnow, along with dashes of vitamins and minerals. Finally, just a few days before I felt the kingfisher was ready to be released, he died. It was sudden and without warning. The bird simply died.

Linda cried. I threw a pair of forceps against the wall. The dent is still there.

That is a very frustrating aspect of treating wild birds. They could look good one day, and be dead the next. There was no time to mentally adjust to the fact that a patient might be lost. Slam, it just hits.

It took me awhile to handle this innate defense mechanism of birds. It was wholly unlike that of pets.

In the wild, birds are constantly subjected to predation and must never appear weak or sick, lest they be singled out for attack. Their bodies are physiologically designed to maintain a near-normal posture and attitude even when they are ill. In this way, a very sick bird uses great body reserves of energy in a very short time. When the energy reserves are finally gone, the bird deteriorates extremely rapidly. By the time the characteristic signs of illness in a bird appear—change in food consumption, droppings, general attitude, appearance, or the onset of labored breathing—the bird is not just getting sick; it has been ill for some time and the end may be near.

That's what must have happened with the kingfisher. I never even suspected he was sick.

Of course we had our better moments, too. Like the time we raised three orphaned sea gulls and released them on the shores of Gitcheegumee. Or the time Linda and I reared two barred owls whose mother had abandoned the youngsters after a logger chopped down the nest tree.

Orphaned mammals were easier to raise than orphaned birds. Unlike birds, most mammals required more than the basics of food, water, and shelter. They needed touching stimulation. We found out that fawns grew faster and were healthier if they were given extra attention. Linda was a natural in this department. She had proven her skills with Faline, our first fawn, and again with Dandelion, our second.

It was with Grizzly though, a baby woodchuck she

raised, that I knew Linda had a unique talent. She was gifted.

"There is someone in the first exam room for you, Ror." Linda handed me a patient record affixed to a clipboard. The only word typed at the top was "Woodchuck."

"Woodchuck," I said aloud. "What's wrong with it?" I took the clipboard from her hand.

"Don't know. She didn't open the box for me." Linda shrugged. "It's Sally Grennier and she's pretty upset. Something must have happened."

I opened the door of the first exam room. A white shoe box with binder's twine wrapped several times around it was on the table. Someone had poked holes through the cover, apparently to allow air to get inside. I always chuckled when someone poked air holes in cardboard boxes. The things weren't airtight anyway.

Mrs. Grennier nervously tapped her fingers on the table. She owned two standard poodles, Rufus and Reggie, that I doctored frequently. Both dogs had allergies.

"Hi, Sally, how are you?" I leaned over and untied the knot of the box. "A woodchuck, huh? Must be this year's to fit in here." I knew that adult woodchucks might weigh upward of ten pounds. This had to be a little one.

"You're not going to believe what happened." Sally's jawline tensed. Her shoulder-length brunette hair waved back and forth as she shook her head. "The neighborhood boys, I could just kill 'em."

I lifted the top off the box. The smell of smoke and singed hair pierced the air. A lifeless baby woodchuck lay curled on a pile of green grass. The fur on his head and back of his neck was curled and frayed on the ends. When I rubbed it with my finger, the scorched hair fell off.

"What happened?" I lifted the animal out of the box. His head moved a little, and his eyes opened.

"Those damn kids poured gas down the hole and lit

it. I heard the squealing and saw the smoke." Sally caught her breath. "Before I got there, they killed the mother with a shovel. This one was able to crawl partway out of the den. I thought he was dead, too, but he wiggled when I touched him."

I looked down at the motherless woodchuck. It didn't appear that the flame had charred his skin, but there was something wrong with his eyes. Rather than clear and transparent, the corneas were whitish gray and opaque. The fire had burned his eyes.

"Well, I'll do what I can, but it doesn't look good. The eyes are burned." I turned the orphan toward Sally.

"Oh, my God." Sally put her hand over her mouth. Tears welled in her eyes.

"If I can save him, I will. But if he doesn't regain sight . . ." My voice trailed off.

"Don't say it, I understand." Sally knew what I was thinking. "I'm going to have a talk with the parents of those boys. That one—Tommy Raddison—is fifteen years old. He oughta know better." Sally was angry. "Besides, what are those kids doing with gasoline?"

"Tommy Raddison, huh?" His father was an accountant in town. "I'll talk to his dad." I was furious. This was not the first time I had seen animals that had been horribly mistreated by teenagers.

Sally Grennier closed the door behind her. I looked down at the woodchuck. He was no more than ten inches long, and that included his bushy tail. Except for the charred black hairs on his face, neck, and small round ears, his fur was grizzled brown with just a hint of red. His short, stout legs did not move at all when I gently rolled him from side to side.

I flicked the overhead light off and shined the ophthalmoscope into each eye. Even with that specialized instrument, it was still impossible to see through the clouded corneas. If I could not see in, I knew he couldn't see out. He was totally blind. I doubted that he would heal.

I put the woodchuck back into the shoe box and carried it out of the room. Linda met me at the door.

"I heard part of what Sally said. How bad is he?" Linda reached over and gingerly picked up the new patient. She gasped when she saw his eyes. "Will he get better, Ror?" Linda quavered.

I didn't answer for a moment. "Well . . . I seriously doubt it. Maybe," I thought aloud, "it would be better to put him to sleep. . . . Of course, it is possible . . ."

Linda named him Grizzly and latched on, hand and heart, to the little critter. She instilled soothing ointment into each eye many times throughout the rest of that day. When Grizzly refused the formula Linda prepared, she supplied nourishment via a stomach tube. I wanted to help, but Linda insisted on being in charge of the burn victim.

That evening her vigil continued. She administered ointment and milk replacer every few hours throughout the night. Linda still would not let me take a turn.

My wife persisted with this regimen for at least a week. The woodchuck would come to work with us each day and back home at night. Grizzly did finally relent to bottle feeding but that actually took longer. Linda's sleep was so interrupted that I caught her nodding off at the front desk during lunch hour.

By the eighth day, I might have given up. Despite intensive therapy—frequent eyes washes, ointments, injections—Grizzly's eyes hadn't changed. He did, however, have a voracious appetite. The formula, and now bits of lettuce, apples, and clover, were wolfed down. He was doing great—except for the eyes. A blind woodchuck could not survive in the wild.

Even though we did our best not to treat wild animals

as pets, it was impossible to avoid some kind of attachment. Certainly Linda felt something for Grizzly. It was unplanned but not wholly unforeseen. I had heard of other wildlife rehabilitators who boasted that they never named their patients or became attached in any way. I wondered about that. Grizzly's chances of survival in the wild—if he got a chance—were not hampered by my wife's feelings. Qualities like compassion, caring, and giving inevitably lead to a special bond. You can't have the feelings without the consequences—or the emotional risks.

Linda cried when I implied that Grizzly might never see again. If anything, it deepened her resolve. There was no easing of her schedule.

After fourteen full days, we got our first indication that things were not hopeless. When I shined the ophthalmoscopic light into Grizzly's right eye, I could make out the vague outline of his iris. The iris expanded, then contracted when I probed the eye with a beam from a more powerful light.

Two days later, the eye was clearer still. I could see the retina. Linda was elated. Grizzly was finally getting better.

It took another three weeks for the right eye to heal entirely. The left eye recovered, too, except for one spot near the perimeter close to the white portion.

An orphaned woodchuck sits up, waiting for his lunch. During hibernation, the woodchuck's temperature drops to 40 degrees, breathing slows to about once every six minutes, and the pulse drops to 4 beats per minute. Abandoned woodchuck tunnels are used by rabbits, opossums, raccoons, and foxes.

On August 3, we decided to return Grizzly to the wild. Woodchucks eat green vegetation—grasses, clover, alfalfa, and plantain—so I selected a deserted farm for his release. A dilapidated wooden gate prevented us from driving the last quarter-mile or so to an abandoned orchard near a former hay field. The hay was overgrown with lush green grass—not enough alfalfa for a farmer, but more than enough to feed Grizzly for years to come.

"That'll be the perfect spot," I told Linda. She scooped Grizzly under her arm and closed the door of the Bronco. We would hike the rest of the way.

"Do I need my raincoat?" Linda reached back for the door. "I brought it along." She glanced up at the graying western sky.

"No way. It won't rain," I assured her.

"Then forget it. I'll leave my coat here." She spun around and followed me down the overgrown dirt road. I kicked the pebbly sand underfoot. It's no wonder this farmer couldn't make a go of it.

A small patch of blackberry bushes stretched along the left of the roadway. The ripened fruit bobbed in the gusty wind.

The sky was decidedly darker by the time we reached the edge of the orchard. Thunder rumbled ominously. Linda shot me an anxious glance. Over to the right, underneath a scraggly apple tree, an old hay wagon rested where it had been left behind. Through the long grass, I could see the heavy iron tongue. It was red with rust. One wheel of the wagon had fallen off entirely. The wood of the tilted bed was weathered gray but would still provide shelter underneath.

Rain, the pelting drops that can wet through a jacket in just a matter of seconds, began falling. Wind whipped across the open field. Black-eyed Susans and purple bergamot bowed to the east.

Linda held Grizzly against her chest to protect him from the sudden squall. She bent down and carefully placed him under the antiquated wagon. Now the rain fell harder. I looked at my wife. It was her physical beauty that had first attracted me to her. Before we met, she had modeled for a time in Florida. I had seen her portfolio. Her pictures were sometimes elegant, sometimes sophisticated, but always striking.

Her dark-brown hair was completely soaked. Underneath the faint veil of sorrow on her face, there was, at the same time, a pervading warmth. I could see it and feel it. There was something about this person. She had hardly aged at all. A little more mascara here, some liner there, the right lipstick and blush combined with the proper lighting, and she would look like the photographs again.

But it wasn't the physical qualities that mattered to me now. Her drenched hair clung to her head. Water ran down her face and dripped off her chin. Her large blue eyes were wet with rain—or were there tears, too? She bent down to touch Grizzly for the last time. There was a glow—a special sense of compassion—about this woman. This was the beauty I married.

ALASKA

THE ENGINES ROARED. THE ACCELERATION PUSHED ME BACK against the seat. I managed to turn my head and look out the window of the Alaskan Airlines Boeing 727. Patches of green could be seen scattered through a gray canopy of fog.

"Looks like we're circling again," I muttered to Bill Stromdahl, my fishing partner.

"One more approach. That's all he's got. If we don't get in this time, we'll have to go on to Juneau." Bill shot me a sideways glance. Unlike the passengers around us, Bill did not look worried. Probably because he had been through so many landings—and near landings—in Alaska in the past. He had lived for a time in our forty-ninth state. This was nothing new to him.

Bill may not have been nervous, but I was. On the first approach I had seen the runway. It was gravel! For a plane this size, I couldn't believe it. We banked sharply to the left.

"This is it. We're going to make it this time," Bill encouraged. He knew I was anxious. "Relax, Ror, relax. Alaskan pilots are the best in the world. Besides, if we don't land here, I have friends in Juneau. We can spend the night with them and then try to get out tomorrow." Bill cheered. I could tell he was enjoying himself.

"No problem. I just want to get fishing." This was my first vacation since starting the clinic in Minocqua. After working seven days a week for virtually two years, I was ready for a break. I didn't care if I saw a dog or a cat all week. No phone calls from worried pet owners. No emergency calls. I was free.

There it was again. That familiar feeling in the gut. We were descending rapidly. The pilot throttled back. I stared out the window. Visibility, zero. I felt it again. We were lower. Still nothing but fog. Abruptly, we were under it. Within seconds the wheels thudded and bounced on the gravel.

"We made it. We're here." My wide grin served as testimony to my mood. I peered through the window. Characteristic of the weather in southeastern Alaska, it was raining. Called simply the Southeast by natives, this part of Alaska was that seemingly insignificant piece of real estate clinging precariously to the rest of the largest state. We had just landed in Petersburg, a commercial fishing and lumber town, on the north tip of rugged Mitkof Island.

Little Norway, as Petersburg is called, had been settled by hearty Scandinavians seventy-five years before. Bill's cousins, Dave and Celia Carlson, were current residents of this isolated town.

I was lucky. Bill had invited me along on his annual Alaskan fishing venture. From what Bill had said, Dave and Celia would make us feel at home. Alaskan hospitality, he called it.

I climbed down the steps. After the confines of the stuffy aircraft, the rain was refreshing.

Bill walked ahead of me. "That's Dave," he yelled over his shoulder. "The bearded guy in the brown coat. Over by the green pickup."

Bill waved at Dave and walked faster.

"Rory, this is my cousin Dave. Dave this is Rory Foster." Through Dave's untrimmed reddish beard and mustache, his lower lip bulged slightly from the pinch of tobacco hidden behind. The right-hand pocket on his canvas coat was torn and hung limply. I could still make out the duck pattern on the exposed red lining.

Dave spat beside the rear tire of his truck. "Welcome to Petersburg. You guys should be just in time for the silver run in Blind Slough." It was September 3, perfect timing for the annual fall coho run. The encouragement from Dave was good news. After all, he owned half of the commercial salmon troller *Quest*. If anyone knew the salmon movements in the area, he should.

"Where's Blind Slough?"

Dave could detect the excitement in my voice. He spat again, this time right on the tire. "It won't be hard to find," he chuckled. "You just follow the road—the only road—about ten miles out of town." I had studied the map of the island before the trip. There was only one road, and it didn't even go all the way around the island.

We loaded the gear into the back of the pickup and drove the mile or so to Dave's house. By the time we unpacked, it was almost 5:00 P.M. Not enough time left in the day to buy fishing licenses and get our tackle ready for use, but there was enough time for a quick jaunt to the river Bill's cousin had mentioned. Dave told us where we could pull off the road and park. Then we'd have about a quarter-mile hike back to Blind Slough. If the silver salmon were in, we'd know it, he said.

Before we left, Dave gave us a partially used bag of Red Man chewing tobacco to share. Apparently, enjoying this habit was a prerequisite for catching salmon or even scouting the area.

Bill and I borrowed the truck and headed west out of Petersburg. After only a mile, we had put the town and its 2,400 residents behind us. Except for an occasional cabin or logging trail, we were in the wilderness.

"Bill, would you slow down a bit?" I began to roll my window down. "I've got to spit." The chaw tasted pleasant but required frequent spitting by the untrained.

Bill complied, and I leaned out the window. The soft aroma of spruce and cedar mingled with the salt air. An eagle lit in a towering conifer next to the road.

"Do you realize," Bill began, "that there are more bald eagles in the Southeast than in all the other states combined?" Bill slowed further and, ignoring the incessant drizzle, I craned my head upward. The eagle shrieked, swooped downward, and was swallowed by the gossamer mist that sifted through and floated above the lush forest.

Despite the rain, the landscape had a fierce natural beauty. The Southeast had been glacially carved during the last great ice age, ten thousand years ago. The region is a maze of jagged and irregular peaks that vault directly out of the ocean straight up to snow. Great gashes of deep fiords score this vast Pacific archipelago. The thousand or more islands are separated by sounds, straits, channels, and narrows.

Bill and I drove on. The road coursed back and forth, first through the thick pine forest and then along the Wrangell Narrows, a treacherous twenty-one-mile stretch of the famed Inside Passage. This is the waterway that provides a safe route through the Southeast, where even the largest luxury ships can travel in protected waters, thus avoiding the turbulent open Pacific.

A dip in the road broke the mesmerizing spell of the grandeur. "Do you think we'll see any wildlife?" I asked Bill.

"We should," Bill replied. "This is a wildlife paradise." Bill was right. I had studied the animals of the Southeast in detail. Now that I was here, I hoped to at least catch a glimpse of some of the indigenous species. Two kinds of bears are plentiful on the islands. Interestingly, the islands where brown bears reside do not have black bears, and vice versa. Mitkof had black. Wolves, lynx, wolverines, foxes, mink, and otters are not uncommon inhabitants. Moose are not particularly prolific, but they do occur in the larger drainage areas on the mainland across the sound from Petersburg. Sitka blacktail deer find the coastal forest ideal.

The warming Japanese current is responsible for the maritime climate of the Southeast. Mixing sea waters, along with the extreme tides, provide abundant food for the marine life. Dungeness, tanner, and king crab, shrimp, and butter clams thrive in the aquatic environment around Petersburg. Five species of salmon, giant halibut, cod, and herring provide the basis for the fishery. Southeastern waters are home to Dall and harbor porpoises, humpback, fin, and killer whales, and several kinds of seals. More than fifty species of seabirds—including terns, gulls, kittiwakes, auklets, and murres—can be seen, along with numerous species of waterfowl.

"Look!" Bill pointed ahead. "A bear." I looked down the road. A black bear disappeared into the underbrush.

"Well, that's something!" I exclaimed. "We've only been here a couple hours and we've already seen a bear." Bill beamed like a tour guide who had just shown his group a famous landmark.

"Alaska—how do you like it so far?" His question did not require an answer.

"How much farther is the trail back to the river?" I asked.

"According to Dave's directions, it's about another mile and a half." Bill sped up just a little. The windshield wipers squeaked rhythmically.

The road jogged to the left. I scanned the roadside, hoping to glimpse more wildlife. I couldn't believe my eyes. I sat up on the edge of my seat and looked again.

"Stop the truck!" I yelled to Bill. "Stop the truck!" The pickup skidded to a halt on the wet pavement. Before the truck had completely stopped, I tried to open the door. It stuck at first, so I jolted it open with my shoulder.

"What's going on? What are you doing?" I heard Bill shout as I ran behind the truck to a clump of leafy sword ferns.

I bent over and scooped up a drenched black and white kitten. His raspy meow was barely audible. "What are you doing out here?" I thought out loud. "You look pathetic." I hurried back to the truck.

"Look at this, Bill." I clutched the kitten and shut the door. Bill's thick, dark eyebrows wrinkled in disbelief.

"What are you doing way out here?" Bill echoed my thoughts. He took the kitten and studied it. After a few seconds, he smiled and handed him back.

The little guy was cold to the touch. I knew the danger of hypothermia in young animals, so I reached over and slammed the heater into high gear. I began to wrap the kitten up in a blue and white checkered flannel shirt that was lying on the seat. "Dave won't mind if I use his shirt," I muttered. Suddenly, my fingers felt something else. This kitten was more than just wet and cold.

"Bill, there's something wrong here." I glanced at Bill and then back down to the bundle in my lap. Delicately, I palpated the right rear leg. There it was again. I could feel the grating.

"You know what, this kitten has a fractured femur." I gently felt the leg again.

Bill was incredulous. "How could he have gotten this far with a broken leg? We haven't seen a house for miles."

I knew what had happened. I had seen it too many times before. "This kitten was tossed from a moving car. I've seen it a hundred times. When some people abandon animals, they just slow down and throw them by the side of the road. That's why so many abandoned pets found along highways have broken limbs. I can tell by feeling that this is an impact fracture. The bone smashed when the leg hit the ground."

"Are you sure?"

"I'm nearly positive. If he'd been hit by a car after being dumped off, there would be some external signs of damage. Look, there's not even a scratch on his skin." I held the kitten toward Bill so he could see. "Besides," I added, "as I said, I see it all the time."

I rewrapped the kitten and held him in my lap. Bill pulled back onto the road and we continued. "I thought you were coming here to get away from veterinary medicine," he chided.

"So did I," I laughed.

I didn't consider myself a "cat person" like others I know. Of course, I do like cats, but no more than other creatures. The truth is, I never met an animal I didn't like. There were some people I did not particularly care for—like the ones who had mistreated this feline.

Certainly, if left in the rain overnight, the kitten would have succumbed to exposure. He had to be rescued.

A little farther and we arrived at our destination. The kitten was warm and sleeping restfully, so we left him curled up in the truck and began the trek to Blind Slough. The path was actually a series of planks stretching across a muskeg bog. With every step, water oozed between the boards. Bill explained that the planks had been placed there by the Alaska Fish and Game Department—a work project or something like that.

It was low tide. Rocks, ranging from pebbles to elephantine boulders, lined the stream. Every few seconds a salmon was momentarily airborne. "They're here. They're here," Bill announced. His voice competed with the outward rushing water. "They're jumping so they can see where they're going, you know," Bill instructed. He maintained a poker face.

"Really? I thought they jumped so they can see where the fishermen are." Neither of us could help it any longer. We burst out laughing. There were several theories on why returning cohos jump so often. We didn't know which was true, but we did know that ours were false.

We huddled on the bank of Blind Slough and watched the salmon. It was a moment to savor.

I reached into my down vest and pulled out Dave's crumpled foil bag of tobacco. "Here, Bill, how about a chaw?" Bill reached over and took a suitable wad. His cheek bulged perceptibly. Feeling the spirit of the moment, I dipped in and secured a generous amount.

Less than a minute later I knew I had overindulged. I steadied myself against a sapling. "Does this stuff ever make you dizzy?"

"You look a little pale. You're swallowing too much. You gotta spit more." Bill leaned over and planted a healthy gob of juice at his feet. It spattered on his boots and khaki pant legs. "See, like this."

I imitated Bill and spit profusely. Soon I felt better.

We were two kids behind the barn. Alaska can do that to a person.

A bird landed in a nearby red alder. It looked like a blue jay but lacked the crest and head pattern. "A Steller's jay," I said under my breath.

For the first half of our journey back over the muskeg, Bill and I discussed fishing strategy.

After a brief lull in our conversation, I blurted what I'd been thinking, "Alaska . . . I think I'll call him Alaska."

Bill stopped and turned around. "Huh, call who Alaska?"

"Why, my new cat, of course." I hesitated then continued. "I certainly can't leave him up here. You know there's no vet in Petersburg."

"Alaska. I like that name, but are you really thinking of taking him all the way back to Wisconsin?"

"What other choice is there? The way that leg feels it'll have to be fixed. You know, surgery. That's about the only way he'll be able to use it again."

A short time later we arrived back at the truck. Nestled in the flannel shirt, the kitten was still asleep. He didn't even wake up when I placed him in my lap for the ride back to town.

Dave wasn't too excited with the new houseguest, but Celia was defenseless. She adored Alaska. Even their golden retriever, Dustin, liked the kitten.

By the next morning, some of the spunk had returned to my injured patient. Maybe it was the warm lodging or the cooked salmon feasts, or maybe just the attention—or a combination of all three. Despite his improvement, Alaska had virtually no use of his right rear leg. It dragged behind as he hobbled on the other three.

I reexamined the broken limb. The break was too high up on his leg for a splint. Repair would have to wait for Wisconsin.

For the next several days, my vacation was more like what I had originally planned. We hit the autumn silver salmon run perfectly. Bill and I caught scads of coho. For a change, we dug clams, trapped crabs, and fished cutthroat trout and Dolly Varden. On Tuesday we made a special trip to the Sukoi Islands, small islands near Petersburg in Frederick Sound, in search of halibut, the best tasting Alaskan fish of all.

Alaska continued to get stronger and stronger. That is, until Wednesday morning. I could tell when I got up that something was wrong. For the first time, he refused food. He was depressed, and his eyes were dull and sunken—sure signs of a very sick cat. I scrounged a thermometer from the house medicine cabinet and discovered something even more alarming. Alaska's temperature was 105! He was in trouble.

The helpless feeling was overwhelming. Alaska needed laboratory tests and medical care in an animal hospital. For the first time since I started vet school, I was the client. I needed to rely on someone else to help me take care of my own pet.

Born and raised in Petersburg, Celia knew everyone in town. She provided some of the help I needed. She persuaded a long-time family friend and nurse at the small local hospital to allow me to bring the kitten in for blood tests and X rays.

I walked into the faded red-brick building at eight-thirty in the morning, a full half-hour before the routine patients were scheduled to arrive. The admitting desk was not open yet, but I spotted a cleaning lady down the hall.

"Excuse me, excuse me." I walked toward her. "Could you please tell me—where is the radiology department?"

The Native American woman stared at the kitten I held firmly against my chest. Her olive skin was complemented by her dark eyes and hair. She was expressionless.

"Could you please tell me where the X-ray room is? My friend here needs help." I looked down at Alaska.

She understood and smiled. "Go through those doors." She pointed. "Then turn left down the second hallway. You'll see it there."

I followed her directions.

"Hi," I said to the X-ray nurse. "I'm Rory Foster. Celia Carson spoke with you, I believe. I'm the vet with the sick kitten." Alaska wiggled in my hand.

"Yes, Celia called me. I'm Margaret," she said. "So this is your little friend." She leaned forward and scratched the kitten's head. Her frosted blond hair fell forward, covering her rosy complexion. "What's wrong?"

"I'm not exactly sure. I know that he has a broken femur, but that happened several days ago. Right now, he's got a real high temp. I'm not sure an X ray will help with the diagnosis, but as long as I'm here I'd like to get one." Margaret nodded her approval. "Actually, I'd like to see the chest and the abdomen. The kitten is so small, maybe we can get him all on one cassette," I volunteered.

The lead-lined gloves made it nearly impossible for me to hold the tiny patient. I secured Alaska's head and front feet in one hand and positioned the rear legs with the other. I signaled with my head to Margaret who was behind the safety glass. The machine hummed, then clicked. I relaxed my grip. Alaska squirmed and sat up.

Margaret took the X ray to the developing room next door. While she was gone, I realized that I'd better ask about fees. I had checked with the airline two days before and the cost to purchase a cat carrier and fly Alaska all the way home would be nearly $150. A loan from Bill would be required for that. I didn't want to borrow more if I could help it.

Margaret came back into the radiology room. "Pardon me, but I have to ask about the cost. How much does one X ray cost?"

"Let's see," she began. "We took one small film. That would be thirty-six dollars for the X ray and sixteen more for the radiologist's reading fee. So it's fifty-two dollars total." She assumed an air of professionalism.

I gulped. Fifty-two dollars for one X ray. I would have to borrow more money from Bill. My mind flashed back to the countless times in my own practice that I had to explain fees to someone who had rescued an abandoned, injured animal.

"But, Margaret," I wanted to say, "fifty-two dollars for one X ray. He's just a cat. He's hardly mine—or at least he wasn't until three days ago. He was abandoned. I was only trying to help. He's a Petersburg cat. . . ."

In that instant I understood why similar things had been said to me. I wouldn't forget—ever.

"Fifty-two dollars . . . that'd be fine," I replied politely. Alaska *was* my cat. "By the way, just so you know, vets read their own X rays. I won't need the radiologist."

"Good, because the radiologist only flies up from Seattle once a month, and he's not due for two more weeks."

I breathed a sigh of relief, but she continued, "But I still have to charge you his reading fee—you know, hospital policy and all."

I didn't protest. I forgot about the money and turned my attention back to Alaska the cat. The X ray indicated that his lungs and abdomen were clear. His ailment remained a mystery.

Margaret placed her delicate fingers around Alaska's body for restraint. He trembled when I plunged the needle into his jugular vein. Slowly the drops of bright red blood appeared and trickled into the attached collection tube. Alaska offered no further protest while the tube filled, a testament to his deteriorated condition.

With the feline patient sleeping on my lap, I sat in a hallway chair and waited the two hours for the test results. Finally, Margaret brought me the report.

"Here, I'm not sure what normal values are for cats. You'd better interpret this yourself." She handed me the blue strip of paper.

Silently, I read down the list. Liver, fine. Pancreas, fine. Sodium, fine. Potassium, fine. Cholesterol, fine. Glucose, fine. Calcium, fine. Phosphorus, fine. The electrolytes were within normal limits. The major organs were working.

At the bottom of the readout was the complete blood count. The CBC showed that Alaska's white blood cell count was 48,000—four times normal. I did a double take.

"Margaret, could this be right? Forty-eight thousand?" I pointed at the figure.

Margaret squinted and studied the number. "Yes, it's right. We ran it twice to be sure. That would be very high for a person."

"For a cat, too," I added.

A high white blood cell count is not really a diagnosis. It's only a symptom, but it was all I had to go on for the moment. In animals, a skyrocketing white cell count is usually the result of a bacterial infection, very often in the bloodstream. Maybe the damage to the tissue around the fracture site had provided the environment for bacteria to reproduce. From there, the pathogens may have spread throughout his system.

"Looks almost like septicemia—a blood infection—a bad one, too." I was worried.

"Whatever you say. Like I said, I don't know anything about cats."

I thanked Margaret for her help, paid my bill, and set out on foot the two blocks to the downtown area. Naturally, it was raining. Seated snugly in the large outside pocket of my yellow rain jacket, Alaska rode along comfortably and peeped out at the passersby. Sheltering his head from the drizzle, the large flap of the pocket served as an umbrella.

I found a pharmacy on the main street, one block away from the harbor. I was a bit nervous when I walked inside. I needed to purchase a prescription drug, and I lacked the Alaskan veterinary license to do so legally.

I chatted briefly with the pharmacist. He was an Ohio State grad. My Michigan State background enabled the two of us to analyze the upcoming Big Ten football season.

There was a pause in the conversation. I decided to reveal the real reason for my visit.

"By the way, I'm a vet here on vacation. I'm staying with the Carlsons, and I have a very sick kitten that I found alongside the road a few days back. He's running

a real high temp, and I just had him over to your hospital.
. . ." I paused. "Saint Nowhere," I thought, but didn't say.
"And his white count is way up there." I showed him the
kitten in my pocket.

"Oh, is that so?" he said sympathetically. He leaned
over the counter for a closer look. "You're staying with
Dave and Celia, huh?"

"Yeah, I'm here with Dave's cousin. We're fishing." I
looked down at Alaska. "Is there any possibility that you
could sell me some antibiotics? I need some amoxicillin,"
I pleaded.

"Why, certainly. Why didn't you say so?" He grinned.
His Alaskan practicality allowed him to bend the rules. I
admired the camaraderie that still existed in this country.

"I can't tell you how much I appreciate this. You're
really helping me out." I was relieved.

"Here, take this bottle." He handed me the medicine.
"Think nothing of it, Doc. Glad to be of help. I hope the
kitten gets better." He seemed genuinely interested.

I thanked him repeatedly.

"Good fishing," he called as I walked out the door.

We did have good fishing for the remainder of our
stay. Of course, everyone all pitched in to ensure that
Alaska received good nursing care and his medicine. Even
Dave was spotted on all fours trying to hand-feed the
kitten.

By the end of the week, Alaska's temperature had
returned to normal. Except for his broken leg, he was
healthy.

I was scheduled to leave on Sunday. Judging from
the stares at the airport, we made quite a spectacle. I had
a backpack, two fishing rods, two Styrofoam coolers full
of halibut and salmon and a silly-looking kitten peering
from his tan carrying crate. Alaska wasn't exactly normal
departing baggage from an Alaskan fishing trip!

"Looks like you had an interesting trip," the gate attendant mused. She looked at the cat.

"To say the least." I chuckled.

"Alaskan Airlines does require that any animal brought on board be accompanied by a health certificate signed by a vet. Do you have one?" she queried.

A flash of panic crossed my face. "Well, ah . . . um, I am a vet," I stammered. I had already been through too much with this kitten to be stopped now.

"Airline regulations require a signed certificate. You get them from a vet."

"But I am a vet! Which is better, a paper signed by a vet or the vet himself?" It made good sense to me and to those in line behind me.

"I see what you mean." She looked pensive for a second. "No problem." She managed a smile. "Come back this way again."

Once in the air, I guzzled several glasses of complimentary champagne. It had been a good trip.

Linda met me at the airport and immediately fell in love with our new kitten. She hugged Alaska before she hugged me.

"If you go back there, will you bring back another kitten?" she joked.

I reached into my down vest and pulled out the crinkled tobacco pouch. I smiled.

"When I go back to Alaska," I paused, "it'll be just for the halibut."

It took Linda a moment to ascertain my true meaning. "Funny, Ror. Real funny." She didn't crack a smile. But

The author relaxes with his favorite feline friend, Alaska.

then Linda never did appreciate my excellent sense of humor.

She did, however, appreciate my Alaskan find. For years Linda maintained that Alaska the cat was the best thing ever to come out of one of my periodic fishing binges. Come to think of it, she may be right.

IN SICKNESS
AND IN HEALTH—
by LINDA

I LOOKED OUT THE WINDOW OF OUR CABIN TOWARD THE beach. Rory had our two-year-old daughter, Rori Elizabeth, on his shoulders. Waist deep in the cool, clear water, my husband would periodically dip down low enough so her feet would dangle in the lake. Each time, she would scream with delight.

Ali, now eight years old, and Mike, five years old, played next to their father. Together the two children would paddle their yellow and blue rubber raft around Rory and Rori, taunting their dad to give chase. When Ali and Mike ventured too close, Rory, with Rori Elizabeth clutching his head tightly, would dash through the water and try to overturn the raft. The splashing and the laughter of my family could easily be heard here in the cabin.

Finding the rustic log cabin was a dream fulfilled for us. When we had moved to Rhinelander several years before, Rory's constant emergency duty dictated that we live fairly close to his clinic—that meant in town. The cabin provided the getaway we all periodically needed.

My husband's fishing boat, tied to the pier, bobbed

gently in the waves. Later in the day, we'd all climb aboard and anchor in our favorite fishing hole. Rory had started taking the children fishing when they were very young. They loved the out-of-doors.

The voices suddenly got louder. I looked past the birch, pine, and maple trees of our yard. I looked past the forget-me-nots that grew wild along the beach. My husband had just capsized Ali and Mike's vessel.

The cabin, the sandy beach on a beautiful lake, the loon out there with this year's chick safely on her back, and most of all my wonderful family—I couldn't imagine being happier.

I opened my eyes. For a moment I had escaped. I was only daydreaming. I looked over at Rory. His frail, bony shoulders slumped forward. He sat quietly in his wheelchair staring out over the lake. The kids were still asleep. It was shortly after dawn, summer 1986. The silhouette of the dock was barely visible through the wispy fog. The fog was like steam rising from the mirrored surface of a giant earthly kettle. It had been two and one half years since my husband's illness was diagnosed as amyotrophic lateral sclerosis.

He had gone to the neurologist that awful Monday, right after we read the article about ALS in the *Wall Street Journal*. The diagnosis wasn't immediate. There is no specific test for Lou Gehrig's disease. Rory had all the signs, but first such things as brain tumors and multiple sclerosis had to be ruled out.

My husband—his body now a mere shell—is totally confined in his wheelchair. His legs—the ones that carried him tirelessly into Moose Springs many times—now can not even take one step. His arms—which used to embrace me daily—now hang limp at his sides. His hands—which could tie a surgeon's knot in a flash—are all but totally paralyzed. His shrinking neck muscles make holding his head up difficult. This horrible disease was even affecting the muscles that control swallowing. Choking is nearly a daily occurrence. Every meal is a challenge. For the last six months, his speech has been failing. Enunciation is impossible. Words come out in a monotone garble. I can understand only certain syllables and only some words.

Rory depends on me for everything. I feed him, dress him, bathe him, brush his teeth, comb his hair, and wipe his nose.

Even now, two and one half years after the diagnosis, we can hardly believe what is happening. Rory was always so healthy, so vivacious and athletic. Not one day has passed that one of us doesn't ask the other if this is really happening.

Our children don't understand. What do you say to your sensitive eight-year-old daughter who asks, "Mommy, when is Daddy going to get better?" What do you say to a five-year-old son who asks, "Why can't Daddy play catch anymore?" And Rori Elizabeth, conceived three months before Rory was diagnosed, will never know her healthy father.

There are no easy answers. How do you explain it when someone is cut down in his prime? Rory has always lived life with all of his might. Whether he was sailing around the world as a twenty-year-old, battling to start a wildlife hospital eight years later, or simply playing with his children, he has always been involved, always on the go.

ALS may have slowed my husband down physically, but it hasn't beaten him. When he could no longer practice, he ran a veterinary direct marketing company he had started. I'll never forget Rory's resolve. Running a fast-growing company is not easy for anyone. However, as with all his business ideas, he made it look simple. But his deteriorating body kept getting in the way. Several times after ALS had affected his coordination, he fell down at work. Imagine the humiliation of falling in front of employees and business associates. Then his speech started to fail. Despite knowing he had a terminal disease, Rory managed the company with an eye to the future—a future he knew he'd never share.

When it was time to leave that job, he moved into his office at home to devote full time to his writing. The canine health-care newsletter for kennel owners, which he founded and writes, is doing fantastically well. In this way, he stays in touch with the profession he loves.

But every day is more difficult than the last. His staff can barely understand him. I don't know what we'll do when his speech worsens. We may have to sell the newsletter soon.

Even knowing that things will not get better, there is at least some comfort in knowing that his life has made a difference. Just last week Rory got a letter from a former employee who expressed her feelings: ". . . the way you continue to rise above your physical and mental anguish and still keep that old fire is the difference between you and other men. You, Ror, have taught me to believe in myself. You gave me confidence. . . . If you're ever down in the dumps—just remember all the lives you have touched and changed for the better—two legged and four legged—even those with wings."

But even nice thoughts and kind words don't allay the despair. We live a life of quiet desperation. Our family is in constant turmoil. ALS tears at our guts. It cheats all of us.

It's impossible to describe the emotional pain of seeing the life drain out of my loving husband one day at a time. Regardless of his courage or attitude, ALS marches onward. No one has ever beaten this cruel neuromuscular disease. Rory is trapped—trapped inside his dying body. I have never experienced such hopelessness. Oh, God, we need a miracle.

I could go on and on about the horrors of ALS, but

Rory insists that I not make a big fuss about it now. He wants this book to be about better times.

The call of a nearby loon shattered the early morning peace. I glanced at Rory in his wheelchair. His head perked up. He concentrated his gaze on an area in the lake just beyond our dock. I looked, too. Through the new day's fog, I finally glimpsed the bird. It was a mother loon with her chick in tow.

She again let out her eerie wail. I recognized it immediately. She was searching for her mate. I strained to hear a reply. Oh, how I hoped there would be one.